FROM
UNKNOWN
TO
UNFORGETTABLE

HOW TO BUILD A PERSONAL BRAND THAT
GOES BEYOND THE BIO

SOPHIE MILLIKEN

MOJA PUBLISHING

www.thisismoja.com

Contents

Praise

'A must-read for any business leader wanting to stand out for all the right reasons. From networking to speaking, managing your online presence and much more, this book gives you the strategies to get known.'

Linda Plant, BBC One's *The Apprentice* interviewer, motivational speaker and serial entrepreneur

'I've seen firsthand how Sophie has raised her profile through awards, PR and social media, including a huge win at the Great British Entrepreneur Awards. In *From Unknown to Unforgettable* she shares the effective strategies that helped her build and scale her businesses. This book a must-read for anyone serious about making their mark and becoming truly unforgettable.'

Francesca James, Great British Entrepreneur Awards

'At last, a book that actually helps business leaders know how to really become an authority in what they do. I love that there are action points all the way through too as it's the implementation that matters. This book is one you'll keep picking up as and when you need it throughout your business journey. It's invaluable!'

Lisa Johnson, founder and CEO, That Strategy Co

'To build a powerful personal brand, you must be authentic, consistent, and genuinely connect with your audience. Your brand should be a true reflection of your values, vision, and unique story.'

Shalini Khemka CBE, founder and CEO, E2Exchange

'This book will become your go-to business manual, filled with real-life practical insights that make a difference in how your brand is perceived and remembered — making you truly unforgettable!'

Alison Edgar MBE, author and motivational speaker

'This book is a practical and motivating guide to unlock the full potential of your personal brand. From building confidence to benefitting your business, Sophie's personal experience and industry know-how give you all the tools you need in one place – follow it and make your mark on the world.'

Laura Kingston, founder and managing editor, *High Life North*

'Personal branding is a hugely growing trend that is un-avoidable and a must for anyone who is serious about their career. As a result, it's often a crowded space, but Sophie's guidance helps people to stand out from the crowd and go beyond the bio.'

Ash Jones, founder, Great Influence

'If you want to be seen as the KPI in your industry, then you must have a strong personal brand. This book gives you practical strategies to explode your brand visibility.'

Daniel Priestley, founder, DentGlobal, co-founder, Score-App and bestselling author

'If you've not invested time into your personal brand in this day and age, I've got bad news for you. People are already talking about you...it's time to take control of your narrative and decide what you want others to know about you. This book is a great guide to doing just that!'

Simon Squibb, founder, Helpbnk and bestselling author

'Coming from someone who has built their entire business from a personal brand using solely organic growth, I know what power is behind aligning your brand with your true values. Sophie is an absolute expert in this. Her guidance and advice will transform your business and your life.'

Jason Graystone, entrepreneur and investor

For Jess, always.

Foreword by Sara Davies MBE

Having founded Crafter's Companion in 2005 and having had the opportunity to be involved in other incredible founder-led businesses and opportunities since then, I know first-hand the value of being visible and having a strong personal brand.

It's having, and working, on my own personal brand that's opened up many profile-raising opportunities in my career from becoming the youngest ever person to join the panel of entrepreneurs on BBC One's *Dragons' Den* back in 2019, to the dizzy heights of *Strictly Come Dancing* back in 2021 (which fulfilled a lifelong dream of mine to take part in the show).

Now, the term "personal brand" can seem a bit daunting to some, but I found the best way to approach it was to have a thorough understanding of who I am, what values underpin being Sara and then to be honest, it's just a case of being myself. The Sara you see on TV – whether that's on *Dragons' Den*, other BBC shows or even QVC – is the same Sara you will experience on Instagram. When people meet me in real life, the biggest compliment I get is: 'You're just the same as you are on TV or on social media.'

For me, being true to myself means my personal brand is filled with authenticity and warmth. I'm always comfortable wherever I am because I can put myself out there, knowing that the version of me people are experiencing is in line with my values and how I want to be perceived.

Aspiring entrepreneurs often ask me for advice that will help them grow their business or get investment. One of the best things any entrepreneur can do is to become visible and well-known within their industry. When you become known for a niche, for me that was for all things crafting, it becomes easier to attract sales and relevant opportunities that support your goals. By building a strong personal brand, you're also building authority and credibility in your industry.

I met Sophie back in 2018. We are both businesswomen from the North East, and when you meet good people within our fabulous area, you tend to stay in touch! Sophie asked me to be involved in her second book, *The Ambition Accelerator*, which she then turned into a podcast. When she became chair of the female unemployment charity, Smart Works Newcastle, she invited me to become their very first ambassador — a role I've been privileged to hold ever since.

Sophie is someone who's built a notable personal brand and really knows what she's talking about. Whether you know her for her TEDx talk, her LinkedIn presence, or her successful PR company Moja, it's undeniable that this book is Sophie's tried and tested method to getting your name where it needs to be. Taking a leaf out of her book is a no-brainer!

From Unknown to Unforgettable is an essential guide for any entrepreneur wanting to raise their profile. The vast range of content is immense and super useful, irrespective of which stage you're at in your career. Whether you're looking to pick up more speaking opportunities, sort out your social media, win awards, start a podcast, or even write your own book, you'll learn how to do it in a way that's authentic to your values and objectives.

Sara Davies MBE, *two-time Sunday Times bestselling author, Founder and Creative Director of Crafter's Companion, Dragon on BBC One's Dragons' Den, www.sara-davies.com*

Introduction

It's hard getting an intro *just right*.

You might've known me for years, or this might be the first time we've met. Feel free to skip to the section that tells you how to use the book if we're long-time pals!

How am I qualified to write this book?

I've founded and scaled several businesses and grown my profile along the way. My success is the product of taking the actions in this book and I know what is likely to work for you, too.

High-level profile wins include:

- Being the winner or finalist of more than FIFTY awards, including North East Entrepreneur of the Year at the Great British Entrepreneur Awards, described by Steven Bartlett as 'the Grammys of entrepreneurship'.

- Authoring two books which have gone on to become bestsellers in their respective categories.

- Hosting two successful podcasts, including *Beyond the Bio*, the inspiration behind this very book!

- Securing a variety of local and national press, TV and media coverage.

- Holding several board positions where I've been able to significantly impact the results of each organisation.

- Being paid to speak at conferences and events throughout the UK.

- Knowing someone who can help in any situation due to my fabulous network. My little black book is like gold dust.

- Being awarded an MBE in the first King's Honours List for my services to business and education.

This is me: the back story

I started my first business in 2013; it was a bit of an accident, really. After university I joined the retail management graduate scheme at the John Lewis Partnership, and I'd been enjoying climbing through the various ranks of management at my local branch in Newcastle.

After a few years, I was encouraged to go to London on a six-month secondment, and as I headed off to the Big Smoke, I knew I wouldn't be returning to the Newcastle branch. Living in London in my twenties was really good fun and the opportunities at work were invaluable. My last role at John Lewis was also the one I did for the longest: I was head of graduate recruitment, a role I held for five years. This position gave me my first experience of networking with external people and exposed me to a whole new world beyond the partnership I had loved for twelve years.

By 2012 I had returned to the North East, got married and had a baby. I was commuting down to London once a week to work two very long days before returning home to work two days from home. This was tiring, but it did allow me to spend every Friday with my daughter for the first couple of years of her life – a very precious time. It was around this time that the John Lewis Partnership carried out what was the first in a series of major restructures. Like most departments, the team I worked in was impacted, and I had to make the decision to either move back down south permanently to take up a new role I didn't particularly want to do or leave. I left.

I looked for similar roles back in the North East but couldn't find anything even remotely similar, or anywhere near the salary I'd enjoyed having a job based in London. A random lunch in York with someone I'd got to know through external networking led to the creation of my first business.

The company was established in 2013 and I began working full-time on it alongside my co-founder in September of the same year. The business followed on neatly from the last role I had in the corporate world; it was a graduate recruitment and employability consultancy. We worked with employers to design their assessment processes and materials and we also worked with universities to prepare their students for graduate jobs.

The first couple of years in this business were really just us finding our feet and putting the foundation blocks of the business in place. We were making money, but nowhere near the salaries we had enjoyed in our corporate careers. I was convinced that the business had so much more potential to grow but my co-founder disagreed. He used to tell me that it could be a nice business for one of us, but he felt it would peak at around £250,000 per year which, after overheads, could be a nice income for one, but not enough for us both. I knew he was wrong.

When my co-founder left in 2017, things changed quickly. He had previously been responsible for business development, which allowed me to oversee operations from Newcastle – less travel, which helped me as I was by then a single parent following a divorce. Suddenly I had to do both roles, and getting out on the road to speak to prospects and clients was top of my list as I needed to increase sales. Within six weeks of being out and about and talking to people, I had secured almost £150,000 worth of sales and was really hitting my stride in business development and as the face of the business.

My co-founder was an introvert. He was confident one-to-one and in front of crowds, but he really didn't like to shout about what we were doing or what we were good at. When he left, a key thing I did early on was to share what I was up to on social media, mainly on LinkedIn. By this time the business had become known for running large-scale assessment centre simulations in football stadiums up and down the country. I would post from one of the stadiums and talk about what the team and I were delivering that day. It wasn't salesy, but it usually had a clear call to action, inviting other universities to come and observe a future event. I also started to seek out and accept opportunities to contribute to industry publications and podcasts where I would share my knowledge and expertise with what was likely to be our audience. This soon gave me content to share on social media in a natural and helpful way. Initially I felt a little uncomfortable to go from being a lurker on LinkedIn to posting two or three times per week. This soon changed when I started to see the results of my consistent efforts.

Fast forward a couple of years and I had really upped my game. A pivotal moment was when I published my first book, *From Learner to Earner*. By this time I had started to see opportunities everywhere, so when I wrote that first book, I also identified the perfect opportunity to leverage its publication by hosting two book launch parties and inviting all our clients, prospects and friends. We held one of these events in Newcastle at the Great Hall in Northumbria University, and another at the Institute of Student

Employers in London. At this point, we were also doing well with awards and had won or been shortlisted for almost thirty.

Writing that first book was definitely a catalyst for what came next. I was approached to deliver two TEDx talks. If you know anything about the TEDx process, you'll know that you usually have to pitch to become a speaker, and that it can be a rather competitive process. I didn't know this at this time but, being a fan of saying yes to opportunities, I accepted the first invitation. If I had given it too much thought, I probably would've turned it down as in the weeks and months leading up to the talk, I became more and more nervous. More about that later...

The combination of the book and the TEDx talk led to further opportunities, including a column in a careers magazine and TV and radio appearances. These opportunities were not only fun but also lucrative. I found that when I was going to sales meetings with prospects I had yet to meet, they already felt like they knew me and would comment on an award we had won or something they had spotted online. This really helped increase sales. One example was when I had written an article about online tests for *HR Review* magazine and posted a link to it on my LinkedIn profile. One of my connections had seen it and got in touch to ask us to create an online test for her company. I ended up pitching to the senior executives at that company and the work that pitch then led to generated income in the region of £60,000. Not a bad outcome for the hour it took me to write the article and the five minutes it took me to write the LinkedIn post!

Another meeting I recall was with a huge utility service provider; it was an online meeting with three of the company's senior HR team. I was connected with two of them on LinkedIn but we hadn't met before, and their comments at the start of the meeting showed they felt like I was famous, and that they were a bit starstruck – they'd seen me all over social media. This made me chuckle as it felt so bizarre, but it broke the ice in the initial meeting, and I honestly felt like they had already decided that they were going to buy from me. It quickly became more of a conversation than a direct sales pitch.

Once I'd made the correlation between raising my profile and the impact on sales and the fun opportunities I was being offered, I simply did much more of it. Sales in my business continued to increase and some of the opportunities that were presented were insane. When I left the business at the start of 2022 (I sold it in 2019 but stayed on), the impact of my exit on sales was substantial. Some clients pulled their contracts, and the budget was revised down significantly as the impact of my departure was felt.

In early 2019 I completed the *Key Person of Influence* business accelerator programme where I learned even more that helped me identify profile opportunities. The founder of the company, Daniel Priestley, used to talk a lot about the impact of becoming a key person of influence in your industry. He gave great examples: Elon Musk and his brands Tesla and SpaceX; Steve Jobs and Apple. Everyone has heard of these brands, right? But who is bigger and who drives the sales – the brand or the founder? I think with entrepreneurs such as Musk and Jobs, they could turn their hand to anything and their audience would follow them. Take Elon Musk for example: his individual social media followings are significantly higher than the numbers for any of his brands. People are interested in him and what he's doing, but the commercial benefit of this interest translates to sales for his companies.

When I exited my first business, my departure came with a lot of restrictions, many of which meant I couldn't work in the same industry for at least nine months. I'm not one for taking a break for longer than a week at a push, so biding my time before making a comeback wasn't an option. I had a coffee with a business friend one afternoon to chat through how to make a smooth exit as she had recently left her first business and was getting stuck into her next venture.

'What are you going to do next?' she asked me.

I told her I hadn't made up my mind, but that I had a little idea linked to how I'd grown my profile and seen the impact on the growth of my business. I told her I thought there might be a business idea in there, but I didn't know what industry it fell into, what type of business. Maybe it was PR, maybe marketing, neither of which I had worked in.

Her response was emphatic: 'I love it! You have to do this. There's a gap for this service and I'll be your first client!'

So that was that. I created a deck to use to persuade some team members to join me, took on a marketing company to promote the venture, leased office space and planned a launch party.

Since then, Moja has grown to become an award-winning, successful modern PR business working with founders and senior executives to raise their professional profiles. We do this on a retainer basis and now have development programmes for corporates and an online training offer. We also have a podcast studio and a publishing division. It's fair to say there definitely was a gap in the market for what we do!

Alongside launching Moja, I decided to practice what I now preach and started my own podcast, *Beyond the Bio*. You might have listened to it; that might be how you find yourself with this book in your hands. The podcast is my weekly show where I, often joined by industry-expert guests, talk about a different element of profile-raising each week. The episodes are short and snappy – around 15–20 minutes – and come out every Monday. I also put out shorter five-minute recap episodes on Thursdays that link to the longer episode and suggest an action point so that you can apply the topic in a practical way that will positively impact your profile.

How do you feel reading what I've just said? Are you having thoughts of, 'Who does she think she is?' Or maybe, 'How did she get the confidence to put herself out there?' Perhaps you're inspired by the results that raising my profile delivered for me and my first business and thinking, 'Get me some of that, ASAP please!'

If so, great, read on.

How to use this book

The topics in this book provide the meaty content that make up the elements of your profile. They are the substance, the work that will show up when someone googles your name. From online visibility to awards, speaking, networking and more, I cover the key topics that will get you known in your industry and beyond.

I also show you what to do with the content you create and how to share it using social media and a few other tools.

Throughout the book, you'll spot key action points. I know how easy it is to read a book and want to do everything right there and then. But then, a day later, you're onto the next thing. By having regular action points listed, you can take a moment to reflect on the learning and **take action** – something that's relevant and will make a difference to *your* profile.

Let's get stuck in!

Chapter One

What Do You Stand For?

W hat are you known for right now? Maybe you already have a niche and a solid following. Perhaps you've been so busy growing your business or progressing your career that you've forgotten to shake your pom poms a little along the way?

Before you get stuck into this book and identify the various methods you want to employ to raise your profile, it makes sense to work out how other people perceive you right now so you can measure the ROI on any time and money you may invest.

You are what Google says you are

First up, Google yourself. If you've done this before, it's worth doing it on an incognito or private browser window to see what pops up for strangers searching you for the first time. If you have a common name, then you might need to include your location and/or your business or industry in your search.

Look at what comes up on page one, under all the different tabs. The first page is the most important, as that is where people will spend most of their time stalking you. It's worth looking at the other tabs though. You might find an image you hate under Images, prompting an action to start getting a new picture out with future content. You might find you have nothing under News, or that what is there is either no longer relevant or really dated, and you would benefit from some more recent coverage.

Are you the dominant owner of your name?

Often when I search for our clients for the first time, we have a giggle at what comes up. I've seen clients share their names with authors, actors, presidents, athletes and even the odd serial killer! It's helpful to see who else has your name and assess your potential for taking the top spots on Google.

If you share your name with people who are way more famous than you, it might be an opportunity to take stock. If your name is John Smith, then you're unlikely to ever be top dog. There are different ways to tackle this: if you're a married woman, you might retain your maiden name for professional purposes. If you have a middle name, you could include that or even the initial. If you take one of these approaches, the key thing is to be consistent across everything. One client I recently took on had three different surnames in use – diluting her content and presence.

Are you happy with what's out there?

Some people aren't happy with what they see on their Google search. This might be because literally nothing comes up. Or it might be that some old news that isn't exactly positive pops up. A friend of mine was involved in an employee tribunal claim that he (and his business) lost, and an unpleasant news story was the top search linked to his name. Not ideal.

Whatever comes up, or doesn't, there's an opportunity to ensure you start getting consistent and current hits on Google which show that you, in fact, are current and consistent. By being proactive, you can knock down any stories or photos you don't like. Hardly anyone scrolls past Page 1 these days, so it won't take long with a little bit of effort. If nothing comes up, you have work to do, and this can be as simple as posting regularly on open social media profiles.

Take action

Google your name and write down what you liked seeing and what needs tweaking and improving. You can come back to this list as you progress through the book and get ideas on further actions you want to take.

Take the scorecard

Another way you can assess where your profile is at is to take my free profile assessment quiz. This takes a couple of minutes and can be done on any device:

It'll give you a score for each element of your profile, along with an overall score. This can help you pinpoint your strengths and areas for development, as well as receive some hints and tips on how to improve.

This quiz can be used to assess your progress as you can retake it regularly to see how much your profile has improved – hopefully, after some very focused action you'll take as a result of reading this book!

Invisible PR

Have you heard the term "invisible PR" before?

It's what people think or say about you when you're not in the room. It can often be made up of a series of small actions that on their own seem inconsequential but add up to the view someone will have of you. This covers your online and offline activity.

You'll no doubt have heard that phrase about being good to people on your way up as you'll never know who you might meet on your way down? I can relate to this so much. As a fresh-faced young graduate, I remember some more senior members of staff behaving in a way that was rude or dismissive towards me. On several occasions, I think it would be behaviour they'd get sacked for these days. At the time, I just bit my tongue and noted it. Fast forward 5–6 years when I was in a more senior role at head office and the way they behaved towards me when our paths crossed was very different. But did I forget how they'd made me feel when I was 22? *Did I heck!*

Another way to bring this concept to life is to think about famous people we think we know, but (probably) don't. I do an exercise in a workshop I run where I show famous faces and get the audience to shout out words they associate with these personalities. I always have a few very topical names, but that will date this book.

Instead, I'll go with those that are likely to stand the test of time:

- Donald Trump

- Kate Middleton

- Elon Musk

- Oprah Winfrey

You'll be thinking of these people right now I bet. What springs to mind? Here are some of the words I've heard: very rich, crazy, elegant, legend, classy, orange, regal, accomplished.

I'd put £100 on knowing who you thought of on my list as you read through the words.

Powerful, right?

Your invisible PR is linked to how you decide to define your brand, knowing what your strengths are and what you want to be known for – so let's take a look at these topics.

Defining personal branding

I actually prefer the term *professional profile*, but personal branding is more widely understood. That said, when people talk about a personal brand they often mean your social media, and I think it's way bigger than that. I looked up some definitions and settled on this one:

> 'Personal branding is the process of **creating a brand identity** for a person or a company.'

As the name suggests, this is a brand for you or your business.

It's simple, but essentially it's how you project your brand and its values to the world and ensure that your target audience knows who you are, what you stand for, and why it's worth choosing you over your competitors.

So, what makes up your professional profile or brand? I'd suggest the following questions to reflect upon and answer:

- What makes you, you?

- What is your niche?

- How are you excelling within your industry?

All your thoughts on these questions will allow you to bring your personality to life.

In the pre-internet days, your personal brand was pretty much just your business card. Unless you were high profile in the media or somebody who featured strongly as the face of advertising, few people would have heard of you. In today's highly public world, where every little action is discussed at length on social media, you are far less anonymous.

Your personal brand is how you promote yourself. It is the unique combination of skills, experience and personality that you want the world to see linked to you. It is the telling of your story, and how this reflects your conduct, behaviour, spoken and unspoken words, and attitudes.

Why would you want a personal brand?

Your personal brand can be vital to you professionally. It is how you present yourself to current and potential employers and/or clients. It gives you the opportunity to ensure that people see you in the way you want. Your personal brand is what makes you memorable – for better or worse! It's your personal brand that helps you stand out from the thousands of other people like you.

Creating a personal brand requires extensive self-reflection, which is a useful skill to develop anyway. It helps if you know yourself – which surprisingly few people do. Most people find it extremely difficult to describe themselves, although they often find it easy to explain how they want to be. This is where values come into play.

How personal is "too personal"?

Throughout this book, I encourage you to share personal stories.

Whether it's in an award entry, or you're speaking on stage, or through your social media – a personal story will add something.

You'll have a firm line on how personal you want to get. I am fairly open these days, but I didn't use to be. When I was in my twenties, I only spoke about work stuff. Now I'm in my forties, I'm a bit more "sod it" in my approach. Topics I'm happy to talk about at length include my experiences as a single parent and selling my first business to cowboys, and all the stories associated with those facts. This might be too personal for some of you, and that's fine.

Think about where your line is and use that to guide you. For me, I prefer to be open as that is how I am in life generally, and this is the kind of openness I'd share over a coffee or a glass of wine.

Know your values

Values help you establish your sense of purpose and direction for your personal brand. They act as guidelines that assist you in evaluating choices in your life. Values drive you and help you commit to your life. Often, the reason people are unhappy in their jobs is because their values no longer align with their work. When you're crafting a personal brand, you must understand your core values because they're the heart of who you are.

A great way to identify what you want to stand for and what "brand you" looks like is to be super clear on your values. You need to consider what's important to you, as we all have different values and motivations.

Ask yourself these simple questions:

- What's important to me?

- What motivates me?

- What are my values?

The answers to these questions will help you work out what you stand for and what your messaging could be. Spending time on defining your values is worthwhile. Values are lasting beliefs or ideals about what's good or bad and desirable or undesirable. They have a major influence on a person's behaviour and attitude. You can find lots of online exercises to help you identify your values, but try this quick one to get you started.

Here's a big list of values

Abundance | Acceptance | Accomplishment | Accuracy | Achievement | Acknowledgement | Activeness | Adaptability | Adventure | Affection | Affluence | Agility | Altruism | Ambition | Appreciation | Assertiveness | Attractiveness | Availability | Awareness | Balance | Beauty | Being the best | Belonging | Boldness | Bravery | Brilliance | Calmness | Challenge | Charity | Charm | Clarity | Cleanliness | Comfort | Commitment | Compassion | Completion | Composure | Concentration | Congruency | Connection | Consciousness | Consistency | Contentment | Contribution | Control | Coolness | Cooperation | Correctness | Courage | Creativity | Credibility | Curiosity | Daring | Decisiveness | Dependability | Determination | Devotion | Dignity | Diligence | Diplomacy | Discipline | Discovery | Diversity | Drive | Duty | Education | Effectiveness | Efficiency | Elegance | Empathy | Endurance | Energy | Enjoyment | Enthusiasm | Excellence | Excitement | Experience | Expertise | Expressiveness | Extroversion | Fairness | Faith | Fame | Family | Fearlessness | Fidelity | Financial independence | Fitness | Flexibility | Focus | Freedom | Friendliness | Frugality | Fun | Generosity | Giving | Grace | Gratitude | Growth | Happiness | Harmony | Health | Helpfulness | Heroism | Honesty | Humility | Humour | Hygiene | Imagination | Independence | Insightfulness | Inspiration | Integrity | Intelligence | Intimacy | Introversion | Intuition | Joy | Justice | Kindness | Knowledge | Leadership | Learning | Liberty | Logic | Love | Loyalty | Making a difference | Mastery | Mindfulness | Motivation | Neatness | Obedience | Open-mindedness | Optimism | Organisation | Originality | Passion | Peace | Perfection | Perseverance | Philanthropy | Playfulness | Pleasantness | Pleasure | Popularity | Power | Practicality | Pragmatism | Precision | Preparedness | Privacy | Professionalism | Prosperity | Realism | Reason | Recognition | Recreation | Relaxation | Reliability | Resilience | Resourcefulness | Respect | Restraint | Sacrifice | Satisfaction | Security | Self-control | Selflessness | Self-reliance | Serenity | Service | Significance | Silence | Simplicity | Sincerity | Skilfulness | Solitude | Spirituality | Spontaneity | Stability | Strength | Success | Support | Sympathy | Synergy | Teamwork | Traditionalism | Timeliness | Tranquillity | Trustworthiness | Truth | Understanding | Uniqueness | Variety | Victory | Virtue | Vision | Warmth | Wisdom

You'll find all these in a handy chart in the resources section at the back of the book.

Take action

Using the values above, write your top ten values on ten separate pieces of paper. Then, one by one, you must throw away one piece of paper by considering which values are your greatest priorities. Stop when you have no more than five left. You might be attracted to many of the words on this list but if you value everything, you value nothing – you need to be able to distinguish between them and prioritise.

Do this activity with a friend or two if you fancy it, as the discussion you could have afterwards could be really interesting, and may help you to understand your responses and those of your friends in more depth.

Now you have identified which values matter to you, you have a frame of reference when interacting with others and posting online. Your values will guide any activity you take in building your profile, and it will provide you with content ideas.

Imposter syndrome

What if building your brand fills you with horror, nerves and dread? It's likely that you've got a touch of good old imposter syndrome. Imposter syndrome is a mixture of anxiety and a persistent inability to recognise one's own success. This syndrome can be crippling, destroying the careers and lives of its most chronic sufferers, according to *The Telegraph*.[1]

The syndrome was identified in 1978 by psychologists Pauline Clance and Suzanne Imes.[2] They believed that it only affected women, but subsequent research has shown that men are also affected. However, women tend to be more susceptible because they produce less testosterone – the confidence hormone.

I often hear my friends talking about imposter syndrome, and it's clearly a very real thing for many of my peers. My own imposter syndrome kicks in when I get asked to do something that feels a little out of my comfort zone. A key example would be when I did my TEDx talk. I know that many people apply for the opportunity to deliver a TEDx talk, and it was always in the back of my mind as a challenge I should put myself forward for. When I was given

---

1. Burn-Callander, R. (2019) 'Why imposter syndrome matters', *The Telegraph*. Available at: https://www.telegraph.co.uk/business/women-en trepreneurs/imposter-syndrome-women-careers/

2. Clance, P., Imes, S. (1978) 'The impostor phenomenon in high achieving women: dynamics and therapeutic intervention', *Psychotherapy: Theory, Research & Practice*, 15 (3), pp. 1–7.

the opportunity to do one off the back of my first book, I couldn't believe it.

When I had that first meeting with the organiser I genuinely felt ill, as she challenged me to talk about my own journey rather than a safer subject. I couldn't believe that it had gone from a work-related topic that I knew loads about and felt more comfortable speaking on, to something far more personal. Why would anyone care about my backstory? I thought people would think I was full of myself to be stood on that stage talking about my business success. I have never been as nervous as I was in the run up to that talk. It seems silly now, but those nerves and huge waves of self-doubt were all encompassing for weeks before I got on that stage.

As with many things, the anxiety I felt in the run-up completely dissipated the moment I left the stage. It resurfaced momentarily when the TEDx talk was released on YouTube. Should I share the link? What will people think? 'Sod it,' I thought. The effort and emotion that went into that talk meant I had to share it, and it has only generated positive responses, so I needn't have been so worried.

How to battle imposter syndrome

- Accept it. Imposter syndrome doesn't reduce despite proven success. It can be managed with time and support but is unlikely to ever go away.

- Share your feelings with your support group, the

people who think you're awesome and will lift you up when any self-doubt creeps in.

- Be rational. Write down all of your achievements – you'll have way more than you think, so ask friends to contribute to your list. Accept that these achievements are yours and that they are built on facts.

Imposter syndrome tends to affect high achievers who set far higher standards for themselves than other people. If you look at it that way, it's kind of a positive thing, right?

Take action

I created a folder within my main email inbox called 'nice things', and I file any nice comments or feedback from clients and contacts there. Every so often, when I doubt myself, I pop into the folder and read some of the messages. It gives me a real boost.

Set up your own 'nice things' folder and use it to beat imposter syndrome.

Now we've covered the basics on what you stand for, and hopefully got you a little excited about building your brand! It's time to get practical. The following chapters cover all the elements that make up your profile and will provide some inspiration that will work separately or together to get you known.

Chapter Two

Becoming An Authority

Becoming an authoritative figure in your industry means that people listen when you've got something to say. It not only validates your business, it also makes you a credible source of influence. It's a great way to get your foot in the door of the right places.

But where do you start? In this chapter, I'm going to give you some ideas to start building authority that will get you known in your industry and beyond.

Sort out your bio

First things first, have you got a bio?

Is it compelling and unique to you? When you start getting more visible, you're likely to be asked for a bio on a regular basis, so you need to make sure yours is always ready to rock.

The bio should be the staple asset of everything in your profile toolbox. You'll need it for public speaking, drafting award entries and responding to media requests. A lot of people tend to either not have one, or it's a bit CV-like and a little dull.

It's a good idea to have a short bio and a long bio. I keep mine in the same document and send that to anyone asking for it so they can choose which one best fits their requirements. If you want to review yours, or you're creating it from scratch, it might be useful to grab a blank piece of paper and answer the following questions:

1. What's your industry experience?

2. What are your relevant academic or professional qualifications, or industry accreditations?

3. What's something a bit different about you that adds personality and is unlikely to be in the bio of someone with a similar background?

Ideally, you want your short bio to be around 150 words, but definitely keep it under 250. My current short bio is 113 words! This is it:

'Sophie Milliken MBE is founder and CEO at Moja Group. Moja works with entrepreneurs and senior executives to amplify their personal profiles and become known authorities in their industries. A multi-award-winning businesswoman and proud solo mum, Sophie also enjoys supporting the North East region. Sophie is co-founder of City Ladies Networking a networking group for women in business running monthly breakfast events in Newcastle, London and Paris. She is chair of Smart Works Newcastle and has achieved huge success delivering the aim of doubling the number of unemployed women supported with interview clothing and coaching across the North East. In June 2021, Sophie became a Founding Ambassador for Every Child Needs a Mentor.'

It's clear about what I do, showcases all of my current interests, gives me credibility and adds a little personality. No one else will have this bio!

Under your bio, you should include:

- links to relevant website(s).

- links to your social media handles.

- links to any relevant media.

Take action

- Create a 'bios' folder and keep a Word doc with both short and long bios that you update at least annually.

- Include a couple of headshots and any other images you like in both low and high-resolution formats.

- If you have your own website or are listed as a speaker on other websites, ensure this info is updated regularly and – ideally – that your speeches and/or presentations are available as downloads.

When you have your bios nailed, it's time to develop ideas and create content about your business and industry.

Many people don't even entertain the idea of writing because they immediately fear writer's block or think they might not have ideas anyone wants to hear about. If coming up with the ideas is a challenge, think about the types of questions you get from clients. Are there any themes? When you are out and about at events or meeting clients, jot down any thoughts on topics that come to mind which you can develop into content at some point.

AnswerThePublic.com is a handy tool to help generate content ideas. Just enter one or two keywords from your industry and it does the rest. AnswerThePublic listens in to autocomplete data from search engines like Google, then quickly cranks out every useful phrase and question people are asking around your keyword. It's a goldmine of consumer insight you can use to create fresh, ultra-useful content that your customers are searching for.

If you failed your English GCSE and the idea of writing brings you out in a sweat, don't overthink it. You don't need to write *War and Peace*, and you can get a member of your team or a trusted pal to check for any errors. Grammarly is a free app you can use that helps you communicate effectively and error-free.

When did you last write a blog or an article? And how many have you written?

If you've had a go at writing an article, then you've hopefully seen some traction when it was published. If this was on a website other than your own, or a social network, then you might well get enquiries coming off this content for months and years to come.

The thing is, like most things, you need to be consistent with your writing, especially if it is a blog on your website. I bet you can think of at least one website where someone has a load of blogs on one page, but they're all from 2016.

Not cool. Consider planning your content in advance to keep you on track.

The ultimate aim is getting a regular writing gig or column for a decent publication. It's easier to snare one with a local paper or magazine than to expect to successfully pitch a column in *The Guardian*, so maybe start out locally and see what you can get. This might cost you a few quid in advertising, but it is likely to be fairly low in cost. Business websites are worth a look too. They are often keen for regular content, and if you stick to their deadlines and send over new and interesting articles, this could be a long-term relationship. Regular, published content is always going to be a good thing, as it'll be seen by lots of people and remind them that you exist.

If you want to pitch a column, make sure that you do your research. Look at the content they already cover and pitch new ideas that will fit their vibe. You'll need to get personal here – no publication will give you a column without you pitching them. So get creative, show them what makes you and your ideas different and personalise your pitch.

Take action

Check out Moz.com for guidance on how to optimise your blog. The site has all sorts of SEO, marketing and social media tricks that will help your blog perform at its best.

Guest content

While you likely understand the value of creating your own content or being featured in the press and media, you've probably given less thought to creating content that can be published on someone else's website or platform.

This could be where you're missing a trick! Creating guest content gets you in front of new audiences (often bigger and more established than your own) which can drive traffic to your own website and social media.

This approach is likely to be similar to how you'd pitch any press or media, but even more personal, as it's probably going to an individual that you would target. So, get familiar with their content and audience and pitch ideas that would suit them, highlighting all the benefits you can bring. Make it about them, not you!

Take action

Pitching for guest opportunities, be it a column, a piece of content on someone else's website or as a speaker or podcast guest (more on these later) should be part of your weekly activity. It's a numbers and timing game – so, the more and better you pitch, the better your chances of securing a great opportunity. Don't forget to make it personal!

Have you published an industry report or academic article?

A great way to establish authority is to create or commission an industry report. If you have a database of engaged clients and/or contacts you might want to do this as a research report. You might even be able to link up with an academic who has a specific interest in your topic and would add gravitas to your work.

Publishing an industry report gives you an obvious reason to issue a press release and generate a buzz around what you've discovered. This could then be pitched at your specific industry press and the business press more generally, and certainly at a local level where they're likely to pick it up. Other benefits include:

- Being positioned as the 'go-to' person in your industry.

- Expanding your own knowledge.

- Obtaining a better understanding of your market.

- Helping others make informed decisions.

You could use AnswerThePublic to give you a steer on the topic for your report, but it's a good idea to go back to what your clients are talking about too. If you can publish a report that's useful for them and that they will actually be interested to read, it's going to create more opportunities.

You could have some fun with launching your report too, and even consider hosting a launch party that you invite clients and prospects to. This would be a super business development tool and not something everyone can or will do.

What else should you do once your article or report has been published?

You should share it of course!

You can post links to your article through your social media and the social channels of your company. You might want to include a link to it in your email footer and your company newsletter, if you have one.

I've had regular columns in a few different business publications over the years. I enjoy writing, so coming up with ideas and getting them written up is something I find fun. I list them on my LinkedIn profile, my CV and in my bios. It provides content I can share across my socials and we also usually include links in our company newsletters.

When I shared a link to an article I wrote for a magazine through my LinkedIn post, I had a direct message from a connection who worked in my industry that I hadn't met before. We had a chat and I ended up pitching to her exec board a few weeks later and landing a couple of projects that resulted in around £70,000 in revenue. There was some luck involved in the timing of my posting and her seeing it, but it was a great opportunity to showcase my authority (then turn it into a decent sale).

If the article doesn't have a shelf life, you can post it across different channels more than once over a longer period. You can also include links on your website to the article with hyperlinked logos of whichever publication it is from, e.g. 'As seen on BBC News'.

Top tips

- Regular content works best. One piece of something good each month is a great target to set yourself.

- Find like-minded leaders to collaborate with so you reach their audience too.

- If you think someone might benefit from reading your content, send it to them. Don't be shy.

Have you built a portfolio of client testimonials and case studies?

These might be on your company website, or perhaps you have them included in proposals that go out to prospective clients. If you don't have any at all, then this is an easy place to start. We encourage our clients to send out a customer survey after they finish each project where they can ask for ratings on various aspects of the work completed, as well as for written feedback on what was great and what could be improved.

If there's any constructive feedback, we can use this internally to make improvements, which is always useful. The scores and positive feedback we get are turned into a testimonial that we then ask the client to approve. If appropriate, we ask if the client is happy to copy and paste the testimonial into a LinkedIn recommendation so we can use it there too. It is then used in case studies for our website, award entries, client proposals and for media. Often, we get new client enquiries keen to speak to existing clients, so this is helpful here too.

If this isn't relevant to you – perhaps you work for a business rather than own one – you might want to substitute case studies for recommendations on LinkedIn. It's a good habit to ask for one and to give one each month, as this is a steady way to grow and keep your recommendations current.

Take action

Set yourself a calendar reminder once a month to look at LinkedIn recommendations. Give one and send a request for one. Anyone on the receiving end will be delighted and you'll get a steady stream of recommendations yourself. Win-win!

So there you have it. Hopefully, I've convinced you that prose is the way to go. If you don't have the time to write your own articles or reports, it might be that you build this into any external PR support you or your business has access to.

Mentoring

Mentoring is a great method to increase your credibility in the industry, while also being a feel-good way to give back. I've had the privilege of being a mentor to several people starting out in business. I've had various mentors along my own career journey and gained so much value from these relationships. My first mentor was assigned to me at John Lewis. I got lucky with this match because we genuinely got on well, which wasn't the case for everyone.

My mentor Dawn used to take me for a hot chocolate on the days when I wanted to quit. She gave me superb advice and I knew I could trust her with anything. An interesting thing I've found as you move through your career or business journey is that you often come across people again. When I moved to Head Office at John Lewis, I helped Dawn secure a promotion in London; when I had my first business, I employed Dawn as an associate. Small world!

I've enjoyed mentoring others too. It feels good to pay it forward when I've had the luxury of support along the way. Most of my mentoring relationships have been less than a year and have taken the form of coffee catch-ups. Supporting founders has been a real joy because I've experienced all the challenges they're going through and can share the experiences I've had, and what's likely to work as a solution.

A key element of mentoring is not to confuse it with *coaching*. Mentoring comes from personal experience, and it's meant to be a long-term relationship where you share your wisdom. It's one-on-one, with the mentor taking an apprentice under their wing. Coaching, on the other hand, can be specific to a particular task. A coach can still be an expert, but they're not teaching you how to think in a certain way, or sharing parables from their career.

Mentoring takes time, but you can agree with your mentee what your time commitment is, and what format your relationship will take. Hearing the challenges your mentee is experiencing will allow you to reflect, share your own experiences, and hopefully offer great advice. As an added bonus, it could provide you with content to share on social media that might help a wider audience.

There are loads of great resources available online that can give you a steer on how to be an effective mentor. I actually completed a level seven certificate in coaching and mentoring a few years ago that I found interesting and super helpful.

If I was to give someone succinct advice on being a good mentor, I'd sum it up as making sure you have good chemistry with the other person. Set clear boundaries on the time available and how you will work together, and always keep your promises.

Being mentored

As a side note, just because you're the mentor doesn't mean you can't still be a mentee. I have a mentor at the moment who I was introduced to after asking someone else I admire for a recommendation. I was specifically looking to work with a woman who has extensive experience in the traditional PR industry, as I knew this would provide a highly valuable perspective on many of the business plans I have for my agency. Be realistic in who you approach and be clear on how them sharing their valuable time and experience will be of benefit to them too. If the person you approach doesn't have the time to support you, ask them if they can recommend someone else they admire. That person could be an even better fit!

Take action

Identify an opportunity for you to act as a mentor to someone else who needs your insight. Alternatively, look for someone you admire who can mentor you. Send that message now and see what the response is!

Becoming an authoritative figure in your industry takes work and consistency, but it forms the foundations of your personal brand. This chapter has given you some suggestions on how to get those building blocks in place; the following chapters will build on this!

Chapter Three

Maximising Speaking Opportunities

S peaking opportunities give you the undivided attention of your desired audience. They provide an opportunity dedicated to sharing your knowledge and experience while learning from those around you. They also give you a moment in the spotlight at an industry event.

You might have experience in speaking, or it might be the stuff of nightmares! This chapter will cover why speaking should be in your profile plan, how to speak professionally and how to get paid for speaking. I've included podcasts in this section as I'm a big fan, and I hope I convince you too.

How do speaking engagements raise your profile?

Get known

It's great for PR and a way to demonstrate your expertise and get known within your industry. Speaking engagements give you more exposure, build your credibility and position you as a thought leader. In turn, this will establish you as a person to be trusted.

Build connections

They're a great way to build connections and connect with your audience. It's much easier to build a relationship with people in real life. You'll also meet other speakers, which could lead to exciting opportunities that you may not have had access to previously.

Lead-generation and referrals

The audience will listen to what you have to say as you've established yourself as a thought leader, making you stand out from the average professional within your field. Clients will think of you as an expert and the go-to person, leading to referrals and future lead generation. It can also help close deals by inviting prospective clients to see you in action.

Make a difference

Speaking engagements can help move industries forward to make a difference. It's an opportunity to get people thinking about how they can make positive changes.

Your speaker kit

Many of our new clients tell me speaking is the most important area for them to see results in. Often, they don't have a lot of experience in this area, and they almost never have all their collateral ready to go.

The quickest way you can establish yourself as a professional speaker is to have your speaker kit looking slick. A speaker kit is made up of some or all of the following: a speaker pack, bios, photos, testimonials, a speaker reel and a personal website.

Speaker pack

A speaker pack is a comprehensive PDF that includes your bio, speaker topics, action shots, testimonials, contact details and possibly pricing. It can be sent out to event organisers when pitching for speaking gigs, hosted as a download on your website and pinned as a featured post on your LinkedIn.

Bios

We covered these earlier. These need to go into your speaker pack and/or as a standalone document to send to event organisers.

Photos

You'll need a headshot to go alongside your bio and for any event guide or listing. It's a good idea to get some action shots from event organisers too. Many events will have a professional photographer on hand who will be happy to share these snaps with you. Action shots go well in your speaker pack – they are also pretty useful for social media posts showing you doing your thing.

Testimonials

Get into the habit of asking for testimonials from any event you speak at. Include these wherever relevant, but as a minimum use them within your speaker pack. A few lines plus the name, job title and company/organisation is ideal. You could be crafty and ask the person to do it as a LinkedIn recommendation, making clear you also plan to use it in other places.

Speaker reel

A speaker reel is a short video of clips showing you speaking at a variety of events. This can be topped and tailed with some snazzy graphics showing your name and contact details. You can host this on YouTube, as you then have the added benefit of being able to include a longer piece of text underneath – with a clear call to action.

Personal website

There will be several points in this book where I urge you to create a personal website. This is one of them! A personal website brings everything together and positions you as a serious speaker. I have some suggested topics on my website, giving event organisers easy options to pick from, but they can also request a new topic.

You can include all the above details and create an enquiry form that goes through to you or a member of your team. We get regular enquiries for me to speak through my personal website. The form captures all the useful info I need to decide if I want to take the opportunity, including:

- date

- location

- audience size

- talk length

- topic

- aims and outcomes of the talk

- budget

Take action

Get the basics of your speaker kit together so you can identify any gaps. If you already have a speaker kit, check everything is current and look at what can be improved.

Speaking with impact

You might be a super confident speaker, but there are always ways you can improve. Receiving some specialised training is a great way to learn the tips and tricks for speaking with impact. Here are some of those tips to get you started!

Body language

Body language has a massive impact on displaying confidence.

These simple tips can be easy to forget, especially if nerves take over, so do a mental checklist of your body:

- **Back:** Think about your posture, stand up straight and hold your head high.

- **Eyes:** Don't forget eye contact! If you're in front of an audience, take in the whole room. If you're delivering a talk via video conference, look at the camera as opposed to yourself on screen to ensure you make eye contact with your audience.

- **Shoulders:** Lower them so they are not hunched up near your ears.

- **Arms:** Don't cross or fold your arms in front of your body – this can make you look closed off.

- **Hands:** Use hand gestures to engage your audience and emphasise your points. Don't overdo it to the point where it distracts from what you're saying.

You have something important to say and know that your voice deserves to be heard, and your audience will believe this too. That's what will make them listen.

Practice, practice and practice to perfect your delivery! Vary your tone of voice to keep the audience engaged. You might have an excellent script, but if your voice is monotone, it will come across as boring.

Take action

Listen to Episode 17 of *Beyond the Bio*, 'Elevate Your Speaking Game' with Dani Wallace. Dani has the most incredible tips that will advance the skills of even the most confident and experienced speaker.

The idea is key

Overall, the most basic point to delivering a talk with impact is to clearly communicate an idea.

Sounds easy, right? But this point is key to captivating your audience.

Chis Anderson, head of TED, says:

> 'The key ingredient in all great talks is that they transfer one extraordinary gift into the listener's mind – an idea'.[1]

---

1. Hochman, D. (2016) 'TED's Chris Anderson reveals how to give a great TED talk'. *Forbes*. Available at: https://www.forbes.com/sites/davidhochman/2016/0 4/19/teds-chris-anderson-reveals-how-to-give-a-great -ted-talk

He goes further, saying that when a speaker is truly engaging their audience their brains will literally sync up, to exhibit the same brain wave patterns. This only happens when a speaker can build an idea inside the minds of their audience.

So, how can you do this?

1. **Limit a talk to one major idea:** Explain it properly. Your talk needs a throughline.

2. **Give listeners a reason to care:** Stimulate your audience's curiosity by using intriguing questions.

3. **Build your idea out of concepts your audience already understands:** Use clear language, avoid jargon and consider using metaphors to explain any unfamiliar concepts.

4. **Make your idea worth sharing:** Ask yourself, who does this idea benefit? Does it have the potential to change someone else's perspective for the better?

Research the audience

Research the audience so you can tailor your talk to them. Find out what they want to hear, and speak in their language.

While training might work well for you and give you tips that develop your confidence, nothing beats just getting out there and doing it. When I interviewed Ash Jones – the guy widely credited for Steven Bartlett's personal brand – on my podcast, I asked him if Steven had received training. He told me no, he just got out there and put in a lot of hours.

I had some training myself about six years ago. It probably gave me a bit of confidence at the time, but now I would say the things that have made the most difference to my delivery have been to have a signature presentation that I can do with my eyes closed, and also just doing loads of hours of delivery both on- and offline. It takes a lot to phase me now, and that has come from clocking up the hours. I still get nervous, but that's not always a bad thing. I bet even Steven Bartlett gets sweaty palms from time to time!

Signature talks

It's a good idea to establish 2–3 signature talks, the topics you feel most comfortable delivering on without much thought, after some initial prep to get them nailed. You can create slide decks for these and update or amend them as necessary for the event. I have a slide deck for my career journey that is twelve slides long and can support a talk that lasts up to an hour. If I have less time, I remove a couple of the slides. Other than headings, I don't use words on my slides. Instead, I prefer pictures which relate to stories. This then acts as a prompt for me to tell each story and makes it very natural, so each time I deliver a talk, it's probably a little different.

Other topics I have in my arsenal are one on imposter syndrome and another on raising your professional profile, which will be packaged up to include this book as an add-on in the future! All my topics have very clear titles and a list of outcomes, making it super easy for the event organiser to see where I'll fit in with a theme or agenda.

Having a suite of signature talks adds to your professional approach, and you can list them on your speaker page, LinkedIn profile or personal website. It helps guide event organisers and is way more useful to them than just providing vague topics that any speaker can talk about.

Identifying paid and unpaid speaking opportunities

There are many opportunities to speak at networking groups, industry events and conferences – the trick is knowing where to find them. You can approach agencies like mine to manage speaker opportunities on your behalf, including being listed on the speaker page on our website, or do it yourself.

Personal website

Use a personal website to elevate your profile further and position yourself as a speaker. This will yield excellent SEO results and help people find you. You can also showcase your previous speaking engagements, which will help paid clients visualise how you would fit within their event. More on personal websites later.

Social media

Post on your social profiles that you're open to accepting speaking gigs. Include some action shots and feedback from a recent event if possible.

Networking groups

If you're new to public speaking, start small and consider joining local business networking groups to get to know the organisers and attendees. Ask to speak at a future event to gain experience. This will lead to future opportunities as there'll be someone in the audience who will more than likely need a speaker in the future.

Use your network! Ask your contacts if they know of anyone looking for a speaker.

Do your research

Look at online conference directories and contact associations within your industry to identify upcoming conferences and events. Ask who's responsible for booking speakers and reach out to them.

Subscribe to local and national business publications and check out the events section. Use this information to build a pipeline for the next round of speaking opportunities.

Know your worth

Sure, there'll be many unpaid speaking opportunities, but when it comes to paid opportunities, don't feel embarrassed to negotiate pay. Your time is valuable. Remember to include travel, hotels, conference passes, etc.

If you're unsure what to charge, reach out to some speakers you know and ask them what they charge. Maybe you know some event organisers who might share this information with you? Having a contact form where you ask for a budget might give you a steer in this area too.

My own fee varies depending on a few factors. I consider:

- The location and travelling time.

- Do I have existing content?

- Will I secure future business from the event?

- ...Whether I fancy it or not!

As a rough guide, my fee is between £2,000 and £6,000, depending on these points.

> **Take action**
>
> Set (or review) your speaker fee. Ask speaker friends what they charge and review speaker websites to get a feel for the going rate in your industry. You may want to include your fee in your speaker pack and/or personal website.

TEDx talks

When I was asked to do a TEDx talk in 2019, I'd never watched one before.

I vaguely knew what they were, but didn't get just how huge they are. I was offered the chance to do two off the back of my first book and just said yes to the first one. There was no real thought to it, beyond the fact it was about eight months away and I'd figure it out when I needed to.

The great thing about TEDx is that they give you loads of support along the way. I quickly realised what a big deal these talks were and got serious in my prep. The book *TED Talks* by the head of TED, Chris Anderson, became my talk bible and helped me understand what makes TED so special.[2] I received regular feedback from the organisers and learned so much.

---

2. Anderson, C. (2016) *TED talks: the official TED guide to public speaking*. London: Headline.

On the day itself, I've never felt so sick in my entire life. The nerves got me big time! Luckily, I had my long-time colleague, Rachael, on hand to practice with me the night before in her hotel room and keep me as calm as possible on the day itself.

The other point where the nerves set in is when it's released online. This typically takes six weeks following the live event, as the footage is edited and approved by TED. Issues that will stop it from getting approved include:

- your talk exceeding the 18-minute limit (there's a massive timer on stage to keep you right)

- going rogue and salesy in your content

- making your talk political or including bad science

One of my clients recently had a massive win when she heard that her TEDx had been selected to be released via TED. This means her talk is likely to get more eyeballs on it, and it has the potential to really skyrocket her profile. At the time of writing, it's just come out and had over 25,000 views in its first day of being live. I can't wait to see what further opportunities this creates.

Even having your talk released as a TEDx is awesome. The founder of the Female Entrepreneur Association, Carrie

Green, currently has 8.8 million views on her talk,[3] and there are loads of other examples with similar and indeed higher numbers.

My view is that TEDx gives you a brilliant speaker reel that you can use when positioning yourself as a professional speaker. It has credibility and is instantly recognisable. You'll get some great action photos for your speaker pack, too.

I'd actually love to do another one. I feel like I've become so much more confident in speaking and I'd enjoy the opportunity far more – plus I always have something to say!

Top tip

When pitching to a TEDx organiser, ensure you follow the guidelines they've set. Your talk needs to fit their theme and you need to put forward a compelling pitch as to why they should choose you to take one of the slots. Check out Episode 3 of *Beyond the Bio* with TEDx organiser Michaela Reaney for more relevant tips.

---

3. TEDx Talks (2014) 'Programming your mind for success | Carrie Green | TEDxManchester', YouTube. Available at: https://www.youtube.com/watch?v=MmfikLimeQ8

Podcasts

Another speaking opportunity I love is podcasts. I'm sure you all have at least one podcast which you listen to regularly – hopefully, it's *Beyond the Bio*! You might have been a guest on a podcast or may even host your own.

So, what is the point of podcasts? Well, you can reach anyone, anywhere, if you get your podcast on the major platforms and promote it well. The popularity of podcasts has grown massively over the last ten years: there were more than 19.1 million podcast listeners in the UK in 2021. This figure is still growing, with projections of 28 million podcast listeners in the UK in 2026.[4]

If you make it good, you'll build a dedicated audience who will come back to listen to each new episode. You can find your niche within podcasts to climb the charts in specific categories and subcategories on different platforms e.g. Educational, HR, Business.

Podcasts are incredibly shareable, making them good content to post across your social channels to raise your profile. They also help to get your name in another feature on Google, boosting your SEO and helping people find you.

---

4. Statista (2024) 'UK: podcast reach 2017-2026'. Available at: https://www.statista.com/forecasts/1147560/podcast-reach-uk#:~:text=As%20of%202021%2C%20there%20were

Apart from all these benefits, they're just really fun to do. You can share your story, make connections with guests and hosts, inspire with your advice and give your take on trending topics to get your voice heard on stories that matter.

I first became a podcast host by accident. While writing my second book, *The Ambition Accelerator*, I interviewed ten impressive women to include their stories and advice. I quickly realised the interview content was gold and repurposed it as a podcast, also called *The Ambition Accelerator*. It's since had thousands of downloads and it's still available on all podcast platforms if you want to check it out.

The second time I became a host, it was far more intentional. I own a podcast studio, which is part of my PR agency. I sit at a desk outside it whenever I'm working in the office. My team kept nagging me to start a show. They told me it was crazy that I was telling our clients why podcasts are so good, yet I had easy access to the studio and wasn't practising what I preached. As is often the case, they were right. I started in June 2023 and I haven't looked back. Hosting *Beyond the Bio* is probably one of my favourite things to do: I get to speak to brilliant guests and ask them questions about their profile-related area of expertise. I learn something from every guest. It creates strong content and generates leads for my agency. Why didn't I do this sooner?!

Anyone can create a podcast, and you don't need the luxury of owning a podcast studio to get started. If you have zero budget, you can record on your phone – just make sure you get the sound quality as good as possible. If you haven't already, listen to the *Beyond the Bio* episode, 'Podcasting Basics' with Lottie Steele. Lottie's our podcast producer, and she shares some great tips on how to get started with no budget.

How to launch your show

Launching your podcast is an opportunity to catapult it into the charts from the off. If you can get it into the 'New and Notable' section on Apple Podcasts, you've smashed it. I spoke to Jason Graystone on Episode 12 of *Beyond the Bio* about this and I wish I'd heard his tips before I launched. Here are some tips I've picked up that I now advise clients to use when launching their shows.

Choose the right chart

Most people want to be in the Business chart. The trick is to choose a subcategory of the Business (or another relevant main category) chart. So for me, Marketing was the most relevant. I did consider Entrepreneurship, but when I looked at the two, Marketing appeared slightly less competitive. As I've done some other things to boost the number of downloads on my show, I find it usually hits the chart most weeks for Marketing and very occasionally enters the main Business chart.

It's fun watching the charts on a site like Chartable. I take great pleasure in spotting my podcast enter the charts in the most unlikely of countries. So far, I've hit the Marketing and (sometimes) Business charts in Hong Kong, Estonia, Kenya, Denmark and Ireland, as well as a regular spot in the UK.

Get strategic with episode titles

SEO should be considered to boost the reach of each episode. There's a great free tool, Ubersuggest, which will allow you to search keyword ideas and questions linked to each episode.

Keyword research will help you choose a great title and help with the show notes for each episode.

Have a party

I'm a big fan of celebrating success as you go, and launching your podcast is something you should be proud of. Having a launch party can be a great way to get your podcast into the chart and generate a buzz around it.

I've seen this done differently, and you'll know your audience and budget, which will inform the best option for you. You could even keep it simple and do an online launch with loads of social media activity on your platform(s) of choice for you, your business and any guests.

One of our clients launched his podcast with a party at his office. It helps that he has a cool office, but he made it even better by inviting some of his guests to tell their stories, followed by food, drinks and quality networking. Another client had an intimate dinner with some of her high-profile guests and business contacts. The call to action on any approach you take should always be to encourage attendees to like, rate, subscribe and share your podcast.

Get reviews

Reviews are useful. They provide positive (and maybe) constructive feedback on your show. They also help more people to find the show and provide a useful endorsement when they do. If you get a lovely review you can create a graphic out of it to share on your social media. Great reviews will also be helpful if you decide to seek sponsorship for your podcast.

Be a guest

A fun and clever way to attract more people to your podcast is to be a guest on someone else's. As someone who regularly receives pitches from potential guests, here are some ways I think you're more likely to get invited onto a show:

- Listen to the podcast! I get pitches that are so irrelevant it's clear they haven't even listened to one episode.

- Personalise the pitch: include why you've chosen their show and what you would bring to the table.

- Add value: tell the host how you would amplify their show. Include the number of followers on your biggest social platform and make it clear you'd share the episode when it goes live. If you have a mailing list and are willing to share your episode with them, say so!

Get guests

The above strategy works well if you want to get great guests on your show, as you might need to pitch out to get the people you really want.

Take action

Identify three podcasts you'd like to go on. Keep this realistic for where your profile is at right now. If you're just starting out on your profile-raising journey, pitching to go on *Diary of a CEO* is unrealistic, but looking at podcasts in the top 50 of a subcategory on Apple or Spotify is achievable.

'The Podcast Pyramid' with Daniel Priestley – episode 47 of *Beyond the Bio* – has some great material on this.

So that's a quick overview of why podcasts matter, and how they are a brilliant speaking opportunity. Above all else, consistency with podcasting is key. Lots of people start them but most give up after five or six episodes. Think about what a realistic schedule is and stick to it. There's nothing worse than finding a show you like that is meant to be weekly, but then they upload shows randomly (none one month, then maybe two in one day). It looks unprofessional and won't help to build a loyal following. The other essential thing is to ensure your sound quality, show notes and graphics are strong.

Turning your speaking engagement into great social content

Speaking engagements make excellent social media content and can lead to articles in the press, both of which help you reach a wider audience than those at the event.

If the speaking engagement is being filmed, upload the video to YouTube and promote it on your social channels. You can also host the video on your personal website. Just make sure you have permission from the event organiser before doing this.

Want to get even more people talking? Your speaking content can easily be turned into blogs, case studies or testimonials. After you've attended the speaking engagement, ask for a testimonial to validate your experience. You can also blog about your experience and provide insight for those wanting to become a speaker.

So there we go, the benefits of speaking engagements, the opportunities they can bring and some top tips on how to come across well. Give some thought to where speaking fits into your profile strategy and set some relevant goals.

Chapter Four

The Award-Winning Formula

The right approach to awards

Sometimes awards get a bad name. You'll hear people saying, 'Oh, that company bought that award to be able to call themselves the best in the business,' or muttering, 'She's only been named "businesswoman of the year" because she's best friends with the organiser.'

Granted, sometimes these people might have a point. There are awards out there which are more like popularity contests, or whose main aim is to sell as many tables as possible at their swanky awards evening. But when you choose the *right* awards for yourself and your business, along with entering the right category, the benefits they bring to raising your profile, opening doors and boosting sales are unmatched. I think awards can be awesome, and

I have some tips you can try right away to win your first award.

Why are awards worth it?

Awards can seem like a lot of work (especially when you've got a million other things to do), but these six benefits should convince you that they're worth it.

1. External validation for your business

When you win or get shortlisted for an award, not only does it feel amazing, it also instantly validates your business externally. Potential customers, clients – or prospective partners – are far more likely to be impressed by someone else saying that you're good at what you do (rather than sounding like you're just blowing your own trumpet).

2. Reputation and credibility

To win a business award – or to even be shortlisted – you need to demonstrate excellence. Award-winning businesses typically have unique qualities or experiences that make them stand out in their industry, which demonstrates professional and/or industry recognition when they win an award.

Awards can also help you to attract and retain the best people –being award-winning suggests your company values excellence and is a great place to work.

3. A (literal) badge of honour

When you win awards you get a digital badge to add to your website, email signatures and social channel. This is "social proof" of your credibility and shows that you're the real deal.

4. Increased sales

Awards are also a great way to generate leads – and new business – and not just because awards success can help you get found more easily via search engines.

Last year I was at an award ceremony and sat next to the owner of an advertising agency based in Wales. A few months down the line, they'd become a client – something that would never have happened had we not been at that awards ceremony (we're based in Newcastle).

5. Expand your network

Awards also give you access to a community of business owners and like-minded people you can collaborate with. It also creates fun PR and content opportunities for social media and other content platforms.

And you just never know what opportunities might arise as a result of the relationship you make. I was at a drinks party for category winners at the Best Business Women Awards. I met a lawyer at the bar who was working for a popular

Channel 4 lunchtime TV show at the time – *Steph's Packed Lunch*. This led to multiple TV appearances for me as she introduced me to the producer.

Another time I was at an awards ceremony in London when I met a fellow entrepreneur that led to a joint venture for a digital product – something that likely wouldn't have happened had we not met at the awards.

6. Evaluate and improve

The awards entry process provides an opportunity to take a step back and evaluate your own business, so you can improve performance and set future goals.

One client we worked with – a successful HR company – shared that entering business awards encouraged her to gather testimonials and feedback (via a client survey). This was something she'd never done before – it opened her eyes to how this type of content can be repurposed in other ways in her business e.g. for client proposals, social media posts and LinkedIn recommendations.

How to find the right awards for your business

While there are many business awards you can enter, that doesn't mean you should enter all of them. In fact, taking a more strategic approach will get you better results in the long run.

While there are many credible awards which genuinely aim to recognise, celebrate and showcase excellence (we'll look at how to find them later), sadly there are also "scammy" ones. Knowing what to look out for will ensure you don't waste time – or money – on entering scam awards.

First off, it's worth knowing that there are two ways to get shortlisted/nominated for business awards. You can apply directly – which is, in my opinion, the best way. With some awards, you can also be put forward by others – in which case the organisers will contact you to let you know. But while it can be flattering to hear you've been put forward for – or even won an award – it's worth being cautious. Doing your due diligence could save you time and trouble in the long run.

If it's a legitimate award, there will be no requirement to pay for anything e.g. your trophy or a table at an awards ceremony. You may be invited to purchase tickets for your team/staff members, but it certainly won't be mandatory. If you do receive an email or phone call to say you've been put forward for an award and payment is a requirement to receive it, this is definitely a red flag. Proceed with caution, as it may be a vanity award scam.

If you suspect an award may be scammy, there are some simple checks you can do to find out:

- Use social media to check for photographic evidence of previous awards ceremonies.

- Check previous winners, judges and sponsors for follower counts and credibility.

- Research previous winners, judges and sponsors to see their content coverage. If in doubt, reach out and ask how their experience was.

How to find suitable awards to enter

1. Check out your competitors/peers

Checking out the awards your competitors have entered and/or been shortlisted for can be a great way to find suitable awards to enter. You can find this information by checking out their website, social media and/or just googling the name of their company plus key words or phrases e.g. [NAME OF COMPANY] + "award winner", "shortlisted for award", "business award" etc.

2. Do an online search for business awards

Googling relevant words and phrases like "UK business awards", "women in business awards", "start-up awards" or "best business awards" can help you find awards to enter. To find regional awards just add your county/region e.g. "business awards North East".

3. Search websites for key industry organisations

Again, searching relevant words and phrases will help you to find more industry-specific awards e.g. "List of digital marketing awards 2024". Combining your industry with a specific business area you know you excel at e.g. "dental marketing awards" or "estate agent customer service awards" may also help you to identify relevant awards and categories you may not be aware of.

It's also worth trying membership and industry organisations, as they may have a list of relevant awards on their website. Some may even have their own awards.

Take action

Do some research on what awards you could enter. Make a shortlist of awards/categories you could enter, along with opening and closing dates for entries. No need to make any decisions at this stage – this is just a starting point.

Creating your awards strategy

Entering awards can be a big investment of your time and energy, which is why it's important to be clear on *why* you want to win awards. This will help you make key decisions on which awards and categories to enter and where/how they might fit into your overall marketing strategy. If you're a new business, your objective might be to become "award-winning" as quickly as possible, as this provides external endorsement of your ability to get results, along with brand recognition in the market.

If you're already being shortlisted and/or winning awards, your main objective might be about entering bigger, more prestigious awards. I worked with a brand-new digital marketing agency whose founder had a long-term goal of becoming a judge for some prestigious business awards. While winning awards is not a prerequisite for being a judge, it certainly helps.

As the agency was fairly new, it didn't yet have the evidence/social proof needed to win some of the more high-profile business awards. So in their first year of entering awards, they focused on entering start-up awards with "campaign" categories. This allowed them to enter specific marketing campaigns they'd worked on – and ones they had a good chance of being shortlisted for – and even winning. Now they have some experience, they're focusing on bigger/more prestigious awards like the King's Award for Enterprise and Investors in People accreditation.

Which awards/categories are best for you?

This really links back to your objectives and what you feel will add most value to your business. You also need to consider where awards applications fit into your overall marketing strategy, and any other key projects/campaigns that may require marketing time and/or budget. Identify particularly busy times of year where you may not be able to devote time to awards entries or may find it more difficult to get to awards ceremonies etc, as this should be a factor.

To determine if a category is right for you, a good question to ask yourself is whether you have *evidence* to back up the claims you will make in your entry. If the category you're considering entering focuses specifically on customer satisfaction – do you have tangible evidence of your success in that area (e.g. customer testimonials, customer survey data and/or stats that show an increase in customer retention or a reduction in complaints)? If not, you may be better suited to a category where you can provide clear evidence of success.

Should you enter more than one awards category?

If there's more than one category that applies to you – and you have the time/resources available – you should consider entering multiple categories.

However, do bear in mind that this will require more than a copy-and-paste job. You'll still need to ensure you tailor each application to meet the criteria and requirements for the specific category.

If you're not sure which category or categories to go for, you can absolutely reach out to the organisers for guidance. You may even be able to find out which categories typically get the most/least entries. With some awards, you may find entering less competitive categories could increase your chances of being shortlisted and/or winning, so it's definitely worth doing some research.

How much time will you need to devote to awards entries?

If you're just starting out with your awards journey, it may be worth knowing it can take at least half a day to complete an application (excluding any preparation work). The good news is there are strategies that you can put in place to make the process quicker and easier – including creating an awards entry kit (there's a dedicated session on this later in the chapter).

Many awards ceremonies are held in capital cities, so you may need to factor in the budget (and time) for travel, hotels and other expenses for you and your team. Some business/entrepreneurial awards also run "pitching days" as part of the winners' selection process – something you may also need to factor into your planning.

Bear in mind that you'll need to allocate time to promote your success on social media and other content platforms. If you're wondering how to do this, I'll show you later in this chapter.

Creating an awards entry kit (and why you need to)

An awards entry kit is a collection of assets you can use in your awards entries, so you don't have to reinvent the wheel with every awards application.

For example, you can create primary or template documents for information and content you are commonly required to provide on or with entry forms e.g. bios, web links, photos etc. This can even include draft answers to questions that come up regularly on entry forms, meaning you may be able to edit and adapt your information, rather than writing every answer from scratch, each time.

Having an awards entry kit can also help you to gather and organise evidence for award entries as you go along, rather than having to do a mad scramble in the run-up to the closing date for entries. This type of content can also be repurposed for your website, client proposals, social media and other types of content – which is why it's useful to have it all in one place.

Ultimately, creating an awards entry kit is about reducing duplication, which should save you time. However, a quick word of warning here: there's a difference between editing and repurposing (which is a smart use of time) and doing a cut-and-paste job (which is not so smart). Every entry you submit should be tailored for the awards you are entering.

What kind of evidence should you collect in your awards entry kit?

Ultimately this will depend on the awards and categories you're planning to enter. Evidence might include screenshots, survey results, customer testimonials, flyers, press cuttings, client case studies, company policies and reports – basically anything that documents impact and results.

If the diversity category of a local business award is on your shortlist and the closing date is three months away, you might start to gather evidence of your commitment to diversity – for example:

- accessibility changes you've made to your website for customers with disabilities (along with positive customer feedback)

- screenshots of some of your social media posts (to show how you've started adding alt text to all posts to make it more accessible for the visually impaired)

- the flyer for the recent staff training you ran on neurodiversity (along, hopefully, with the local press article).

I'll share more on the types of evidence you can include later in this chapter.

However, before you start drafting awards applications it's helpful to understand more about how the judging process works. This will give you a better idea of what kind of evidence judges are looking for.

Take action

Decide on your final awards entries shortlist and start compiling your awards entry kit (including key deadlines) and documents you may need for your entries.

Crafting an effective awards entry to increase your chances of success

We've all got that friend who loves giving it the big talk about their achievements but isn't quite so bold when you challenge them for proof. The same applies if you want to win an award: you need solid evidence to back up your claims! And sheep don't win awards – in other words, you need to be a leader, not a follower.

In this section, I'll share how to craft an effective awards entry and increase your chances of success. I've broken it down into four key steps and there is a checklist you can use with the resources that go alongside this book, to ensure you don't miss anything.

Step 1: Read the awards criteria and choose your categories

Most awards criteria state clearly what the judges are looking for and what makes you eligible. Check this carefully to ensure that:

- you'll be able to provide the evidence needed to back up your claims

- you're actually eligible for the award/category

- you've chosen the most relevant category for you

Checking you're actually eligible is really important. If you miss something here, you could end up wasting a lot of time and resources.

I touched on this earlier, but the types of things to watch out for are:

- turnover threshold (yours may be too high or too low)

- company type (it may only be open to limited companies, for example)

- eligibility for people/businesses who've won the award/category before

- requirements that you're based in a specific region

- sector/industry criteria

If in doubt, ask the awards organiser. They really won't mind you reaching out to ask questions or clarify details – or certainly they shouldn't!

Check if you think there may be any potential conflicts of interests around you entering a particular award or category, and if there are any restrictions around this in the awards criteria. Potential conflicts of interest might include knowing one or more of the judges or your company being a sponsor of the awards (or being involved in some other way). You might feel silly raising a potential conflict of interest but it's better to ask the question than to invest time and resources into your entry only to be disqualified further down the line. As with anything like this, it's generally best to get a written response to your request. That way, should a problem arise further down the line, you'll have written proof that you raised a potential problem/issue – and of the response you were given.

Step 2: Research judges (and judging)

Once you're clear on which awards and categories are best for you to enter, it's worth doing some research on the judges. While you may not be able to find out which judges will be looking at the entries in your category, you should be able to find out who the judges are overall – which may be helpful. If you're not sure how to work out who the judges are, some awards publish profiles of the judges on their websites, and you can also ask the event organiser.

Doing some research on the judges' backgrounds/interests can be useful intelligence for your awards entry. For example, if you're a single parent running a business – and this is something one of the judges has written and talked about online (or even mentioned in their bio) – this is something you might want to mention in your application.

What you're effectively doing here is matching your experience to the judges, as you might do in a job application. So look out for any connections or parallels e.g. attending the same university, being from the same town or sharing an interest, as this may be useful for your application.

It may also be worth looking at what the judges wrote about previous winners of the awards and/or category you are looking to enter. This will give you an insight into the kind of qualities, evidence and stories they're looking for.

Step 3: Gather evidence for award entries and client testimonials

Before you start to fill out your entry form, it's a good idea to sit down with the entry criteria and a highlighter pen and identify any specific skills, qualities and experience you're required to demonstrate in your entry.

Next, make a list of bullet points of the evidence you can provide to meet the criteria for the category at hand – and any you might need to obtain. I've already shared many examples of the kind of evidence you can include in an awards entry, but here's a quick overview:

- statistics from customer or staff satisfaction surveys that demonstrate a key outcome e.g. increased retention or positive team culture

- results from projects e.g. reports, surveys and client case studies that provide social proof of the results you've achieved

- financial information that demonstrates your growth and stability as a business

- analytics/metrics that validate the impact of a project or resource you've created

- marketing materials (including audio or video content) that demonstrate impact or other key metrics

- business plans or strategies that show you've achieved KPIs or other goals

- client stories and testimonials

- personal stories

Client stories and testimonials are like gold dust for judges. They demonstrate what your customers and clients really think about you, so include these throughout your entry, wherever relevant. Don't be afraid to share relevant personal stories as they can be really powerful and make your awards entry stand out a mile.

You can also add your strongest endorsements to a supporting document and include this as evidence (just check the awards criteria first to ensure supporting documents are allowed and how they should be submitted).

Also, consider the ease with which your supporting information can be accessed and follow the guidance in the entry criteria carefully. While awards organisers will often stipulate the size and format of any supporting documents, common sense does apply here. Avoid sending large video files or PDFs that take ages to download, or content that is difficult to access for any reason.

Take note of any instructions around how supporting information should be sent. For example, an awards organiser may stipulate the use of a particular file sharing tool like WeTransfer. Follow these instructions carefully; if you don't, your entry could be rejected. While it makes sense to use password protection for commercially sensitive information, make sure you've tested it actually works before you submit your entry.

A word of warning: while judges love to see facts, figures and evidence (including testimonials and customer stories) to back up the statements in an awards entry, make sure the evidence you're providing is actually an answer to an awards entry question (rather than information you want to give). So while you may have some amazing data and customer success stories, if they're not linked to the point you're making or to the awards criteria, they won't do you any favours!

Don't fill your award entry with corporate drivel and jargon – there needs to be substance to what you share (and it needs to be authentic and honest). This means you *can* include the "downs" as well as the "ups" in your business (and your life, if that's relevant to your business). What judges will be interested in is how you've overcome some of those challenges, the solutions you've put in place and what you've learned from the experience.

It can be helpful to imagine what the judges might write about you in their winners' summary (which is likely to be a story that inspires and motivates other entrepreneurs and business owners).

Step 4: Do a pre-submission check of your awards entry

It's generally not a good idea to leave submission of your awards entry until deadline day. If you aim to submit your application a few days ahead of the deadline, you'll still have time to spot – and fix – any mistakes in the proof-reading process. Contact the organisers if you have any problems submitting your entry or uploading the supporting documents.

It's also well worth getting at least one other person (ideally someone who has not been closely linked with the application) to read it through in case you've missed anything.

> **Take action**
>
> Start gathering some of the evidence listed above for award entries. Add this to your awards entry kit.

How to promote your award success online

You don't have to actually win an award to promote your success and take advantage of the opportunity to grow your visibility. Being shortlisted for an award is a win in itself, so make sure you don't miss out on the chance to promote your business!

I'm going to show you how to make the most of your awards nominations and wins, including ideas and suggestions of what to post on social media and your other content platforms (e.g. your email newsletter) to increase your visibility. I've also included a dedicated section on how to use awards nominations/wins to generate press coverage for your business.

It goes without saying that you need to promote your award win everywhere – and that doesn't just mean adding your winners' badge to your website. It also means adding it to all your communications and marketing assets, including your email signature, marketing brochures and pitch and proposal decks. You should also add 'award-winning' to the copy on your website, social media and other content platforms, along with any other communications you send out regularly e.g. speaker bios, press releases, etc.

Sharing your awards success on social media

You may know this already – if so, please humour me for a few seconds! – but when it comes to promoting awards nominations and wins, it's worth knowing how the social media algorithm works. This can help you get more eyes on your content.

The way social media works is this: the more people who engage with your content, the more people it will be shown to. That means more people are likely to visit your profile to find out more about what you do.

So, when posting on social media about your awards nominations and wins you should always aim to tag other relevant people and accounts – for example, other nominees in your category, sponsors and organisers. This will encourage more comments and engagement on your posts and give the algorithm a boost.

Promotional post ideas

Here are some ideas for social media posts to promote your awards nominations and wins:

1. Before you enter an award

Consider posting a "shout-out" for the awards and tag the organisers, sponsors and/or judges (and any other key stakeholders). While it might seem counterintuitive to (effectively) let your competitors know about your entry, the organisers will appreciate your support and, if you're confident in the work you're doing and your ability to submit a great entry, why worry about other people?

2. If/when you're shortlisted for an award

Post about being shortlisted on social media (again tagging awards organisers, judges, other nominees and stakeholders). Again, while it may seem counterintuitive to promote other nominees and/or competitors, this is a public demonstration of your generosity and willingness to collaborate (all attractive qualities to event organisers, sponsors – and even prospective clients!) Of course, the more people who like and comment on your posts, the more people will see them.

3. If you're attending an awards ceremony (or a judging event)

This is another opportunity to raise your profile and generate engagement with your content. This is a great chance to share pics of you and your team dressed up in your glad rags and snap photos of you with judges, sponsors and other key stakeholders.

4. If you win an award

This is a great opportunity to promote your business brand online, so share photos of you receiving your award and other highlights from the ceremony. Don't forget to tag people!

5. If you don't win an award you were shortlisted for

This is still a content opportunity for your business. No one likes sour grapes, so congratulate the winners, thank the organisers, sponsors, judges and other key stakeholders (and tag them all, of course!)

6. Follow up after the awards ceremony

Email the awards organisers to thank them for the awards (and the ceremony, if there was one) and to share any positive takeaways from the experience. Even if you didn't win, your feedback may still be valuable (and will be appreciated by the event organisers). If you manage to generate some press coverage (more on this coming up) this is another content opportunity, so share this online too.

If you have the time, there are many more posts you can make about your awards journey – in fact, you can even repurpose some of the answers from your entry form into social media posts – but this should give you plenty of ideas to get started with.

You can also email your mailing list and let your subscribers know about your success. You don't necessarily need to start from scratch, you can always repurpose your social media posts.

Take action

Finding time to create social media posts and other promotional content can be challenging when you're busy entering and (hopefully!) being nominated for and winning awards. Creating drafts and templates for these types of posts ahead of time can make this easier.

What to do if you don't win

While it can be disappointing to enter an award and not win – you may be tempted to crawl away and lick your wounds – taking the opportunity to ask for feedback can increase your chances of awards success in the future. The days and weeks following the winners' announcements are the perfect time to do this. But what's the best way to ask for this kind of feedback?

One of the most useful things you can do immediately after the winners' announcements is to look at what the judges and organisers have said about the winning entries. Many awards organisers publish this on their social media channels and websites. You may also be able to pick this kind of information up from media coverage of the awards.

This can be crucial, as it will help you to understand where the winning entrants may have had the edge on you or your business, and what you can do next time to create a stronger entry.

Ask the organisers for feedback too. I'd recommend sending an email the day after the event, thanking them for organising the awards and ceremony and sharing how and why you found the experience valuable. You can also ask if they have time for a quick phone call to share some feedback with you about your entry. If you want someone to give up their time to help you, you can show your appreciation by offering something that may be of value to them – for example, offering to promote the awards on social media when entries open again.

It may also be worth reaching out to the winners to congratulate them and ask if they would be willing to have a quick call with you to share any tips for the future. However, before you do this, it's probably worth checking to see if winners are allowed to enter the same categories again the following year (many awards organisers don't allow this).

If they aren't allowed to enter next year, they may be happy to share their advice (and feel flattered that you asked). If not, it may feel as if you're asking them to share their "secret sauce" – tread carefully in the first instance.

Bear in mind that successful people tend to get approached regularly by people who want to pick their brains, and they don't necessarily want to pay for that advice.

So, if you're reaching out to awards winners, it's worth acknowledging their time is valuable and letting them know you're happy to return the favour if you can. However, you can lay the groundwork for this type of request by tagging award winners into social media posts. If you've already shown your support and appreciation on social media, this is unlikely to have gone unnoticed.

Finally, if there's an award you're really keen to win in the future, make sure you get key deadlines in your diary straight away, including when entries will next be open. Make a diary note to reach out and ask the awards organiser questions around this time (e.g. which categories may be best for you to enter). Remember to promote the awards on your social media accounts. This is a time when awards organisers will be keen to encourage entries, meaning your input will be well appreciated.

Take action

If you've already entered for an award and were unsuccessful, reach out to the organisers and ask for feedback. Even if the awards were months ago, the organisers should still have any relevant feedback and comments on file. What do you have to lose?

There you have it, *almost* everything I know about awards! I hope it's got you thinking about how they might work for you. If you're new to awards, I think you'll be surprised by how many opportunities being shortlisted and attending events will bring.

Chapter Five

Media Mastery: Success With The Press

If you're featured in print and online media, people have a much easier time finding you. This includes your future boss or clients. As well as the coverage, media features build your authority by positioning you as a voice that is respected in your specialist areas.

I'll show you what to do when approaching the press and how to do this effectively. You've probably realised I'm a big fan of books, so I've included some advice about how to get started with writing and publishing your book too.

Why should the media be your friends?

Being featured in print and online media helps people find you. They will be impressed to see your name in print, and the SEO benefits will bring business and opportunities your way.

Picture this: Your company smashes its targets, hires new staff or releases an innovative new product or service. Or you achieve something amazing personally – start a new charity role, win a big award – whatever it may be. If you don't shout about it, what's going to happen? Well, not a lot really, as your audience won't hear about it. So, what happens if you get the story out there and get featured in the media? Lots of things:

- your name gets out there and your brand awareness grows

- you can position yourself as an industry expert, increasing your credibility and authority

- you establish yourself as a thought leader

- you generate conversation

- you increase your exposure, which means you reach a new audience full of new clients

Getting recognition in the media gives you a chance to lead by example, reach out to others and give your business and employees new opportunities. Every feature is a way to get people talking. Getting people talking raises your profile and gets you known.

How to get started

- Start small and build up.

- Build and nurture press relationships.

- Keep your contacts up to date.

- Track your features.

- Consider all forms of media: online, print, radio, TV and free and paid advertising.

If you're new to navigating the media, start small and build up. Are there any local publications where you can get featured? Local news outlets are always looking for stories and will be pleased to feature local people to shout about their successes – this can include local newspapers in print and digital. Invest time in building relationships with your local newspapers and magazines. Follow their social profiles to stay in the loop on the types of articles they feature or any events they're hosting or attending.

Local publications often have online portals where you can self-publish stories for free. Submit your story, checking you meet their guidelines. Once they're approved, you've been featured in the press. It's great content to share and get your name known in the local community.

One example of a national online portal where you can self-publish is Bdaily. If you're not familiar with Bdaily, create an account and register for their daily updates – these can be for your region and nationally. You can get your stories featured and send updates about your business, e.g. if you hire new staff or launch a new product.

As you get featured more, you can catch the eye of bigger or national publications. Build a portfolio of features to give you credibility when you're ready to go national. Along the way, keep a contacts list and continue adding to it as your coverage grows and you form more contacts. This list will be invaluable for making approaches and sending out press releases. If you don't have any contacts, get researching the websites of local news outlets or relevant industry publications to build your list.

Consider creating a media coverage report to track your ROI with different media and press efforts. A simple way to do this yourself is creating an Excel spreadsheet. Set goals, define your metrics and measure them after different press features. For example, you can track how things like website visitors and social followers might grow after coverage and measure any leads which come from different features. For a more sophisticated media coverage report, use websites like Coverage Book, which will showcase and share the impact of your PR efforts by creating a report for you.

There are many different media outlets you can approach, so make sure you consider them all. Don't just think of the media as being featured in newspapers or magazines. Remember other outlets like TV and radio, which can be an even better opportunity to showcase your full personality, rather than just words in print.

I've had a few great opportunities with press and media. Probably my favourite things to do are live TV or radio. I enjoy the pressure of a situation in which anything can happen, and the adrenaline rush when you go live. I've done a few live pieces of TV: I've been a guest on a BBC 2 business programme and also on Channel 4's *Steph's Packed Lunch*. These came about through introductions, and I was quick to respond with the info the producers wanted.

I joined a BBC 50/50 diversity cohort a few years ago where their aim was to get a variety of UK voices on their shows. This has led to a regular stint on BBC Radio 5's *Wake Up to Money* which has the added benefit of being turned into a podcast. I've also become a bit of a go-to for local radio. Producers know I will respond quickly if I can and that I can talk confidently about most things with little to no preparation – ideal for breaking stories.

Take action

Do your research and identify three to five publications you'd love to feature on or in. See if you can find the relevant journalist or producer and craft a personal pitch to each one. You may want to spread these out over a week so you can dedicate proper time to make each one as compelling as possible.

The art of the press release

So, you've got a story that you want to get featured in the press. You're going to write a press release and send it to some journalists. Before you even start writing your press release, create your list of PR contacts. Have this in mind as you write – the audience should affect how you position your story and the information you include.

Now start writing. The key to a good press release is being succinct – it should be no longer than two pages. Get to the point and make it easy for the person you're sending it to use it and understand it. I know that journalists are incredibly busy people whose inboxes overflow with requests. Make yours stand out with a clear headline and body, so they don't have to do any extra work to understand what your story is all about.

Here's my step-by-step guide to writing an impactful press release:

- Date your press release at the top. Make sure this is recent, as no journalist will want to publish old news.

- Take time to craft a concise but newsworthy headline. This is your opportunity to hook the journalist (and eventually the reader).

- Start with a clear news hook. Think of what makes your story worth talking about and distil this into compelling copy.

- Craft short paragraphs. This will force you to write concisely, follow a logical order and only include the necessary information for the story. Short paragraphs also make it easier for journalists to make any edits they may need to.

- Steer clear of using jargon (or, if you do have to use any technical terms, explain them succinctly).

- Always include at least one quote. This can be from someone who is involved in the story, or another credible voice who can endorse it. Read quotes aloud to ensure they sound like someone speaking, which will bring personality through.

- If you want to include any photos, issue these as an attachment with the press release (don't directly embed photos in the press release).

- Conclude your press release with a clear call to action and any key messages you want the reader to take away. Depending on your story, this could be visiting your website, details of an upcoming event, or product information (but be careful not to make this too salesy as that can be off-putting for a journalist).

- Include contact details for any media enquiries.

- Include a 'notes to editors' section, which can feature bullet points with background information on your business that isn't vital for the main story.

- Don't send it as an attachment. Journalists hate attachments, so send it within the email itself if possible (unless your covering pitch is so hot that you know they'll open it).

Overall, you want your press release to meet the following aims:

- Inform the reader of your story.

- Educate them on your point. What message do you want them to take away?

- Entice the reader to want to learn more, so they take an action, such as visiting your website after reading the story.

Media assets

Presenting yourself in front of the media can be daunting. The best way to approach it may sound clichéd, but it's true – be yourself! Whether writing your own material to send to the media, being interviewed or featuring on camera, don't shy away from the spotlight and use the opportunity to showcase all you have to offer. To make the most of media opportunities, you need to create some assets.

Media teaser

Make sure you have a media teaser in your resources. This is invaluable for building your relationships with the media and helps you present yourself consistently across different outlets. A media teaser is a one-page document to summarise who you are for the journalists who are writing about you, or the presenters who are introducing you. It should include a short biography, notable achievements, commendations or award wins, and all of your contact details and social handles. In short, it's a document to showcase your personal brand on one page.

Media pack

Alongside your media teaser, have a comprehensive longer biography and headshot ready to. It's also a good idea to have a list of your social media profiles, website and contact details. If you have an impressive number of social media followers or mailing list subscribers, you should definitely add this detail. When sending these attachments out, if it's a new approach or relationship, be careful with how far you push, but wherever you can, maximise the opportunity to get your profile out there!

It takes time to craft a story, write a press release, or complete an interview. Make the most of the time you spend on these things, share them across your different social media platforms and keep a list of your features so you can grow your portfolio and your credibility. Sharing media features on social media gets excellent engagement and also yields SEO benefits to get your name further up Google's rankings.

Top tips for making the most of media opportunities

Be prepared

Have a bank of resources ready to go. This includes your media teaser or pack, biography and headshots. Practise an elevator pitch to present yourself in the best light when meeting journalists or when pitching to them over email.

Get Qwoted

Register for Qwoted, who will send you regular journalist requests for your areas of expertise. The free package will provide you with three opportunities per month to pitch to journalists.

Attend networking events and connect afterwards

Journalists will usually attend local events; certain publications may even host their own. Attend these to make connections with journalists and be sure to connect with them via email or LinkedIn afterwards to add them to your contacts list. You never know when you'll have a news story to share, so it's important to build relationships ready for when you need them. Turns out journos love a bit of Twitter (also referred to as X) so make sure you're connecting with them there. I've snared a few articles from being quick to respond to journalist requests on Twitter. The hashtag #journorequest is a good one to follow.

Make it meaningful

No one wants to read a pointless story, and you definitely don't want to be the person writing it. Being featured in the media is great, but make sure you're putting news out that's purposeful and makes a positive impact. Don't flood channels with your stories – there may be such a thing as overexposure if you approach the media with the wrong mindset.

Make life easy for your media contacts

As I've said, journalists are busy people. Make it as easy as possible for them to feature you by preparing articles, checking spelling and grammar, and sending any relevant supporting images.

Use your existing contacts

Do you have a friend who always seems to be in news? Have a chat with them about the approaches they take. They may even be able to introduce you to their contacts.

Aim big, don't forget to think small

Build up a portfolio of media content to get featured in the big time. When you do get to the stage of national press coverage – big TV features, etc. – don't neglect local publications as these are still an excellent opportunity to reach your audience.

Make it personal

Thinking about social media, are you more inclined to follow a company, or the person leading that company? The answer is most likely the person. Take this approach with you when thinking about media. People like to read about people, so let your personality shine. Inspire with your story. Use features in the media to raise your personal profile and get known.

The power of authoring a book

Another form of media not to overlook is publishing. Writing a book not only makes you an authoritative voice on a subject, but it also opens up so many further opportunities.

A sometimes-overlooked benefit of writing a book is that it increases a business's value by making it easier to sell your services, because you become a published thought leader. A book is also a fantastic marketing tool to drive inbound sales enquiries.

This is my third book, and not only do I enjoy writing them, but they have also generated business and fun opportunities. After my first, I was offered a column in a careers' magazine, two TEDx talks and an ambassador role for a national charity. I turned the video interviews from my second book into a podcast series – search *The Ambition Accelerator* to listen – that still enjoys regular downloads. Both books have been sold in bulk on their own or alongside speaking engagements, and I'm hoping this book you're holding right now creates some magic of its own!

You don't need to secure a book deal with a publisher or spend loads of money on publishing. One of my mates,

Dan Kelsall, wrote one of his books (F*cking Good Content) in a weekend and uploaded it to Amazon. He has a solid following on LinkedIn, and its sold thousands of copies and had over 200 reviews!

Planning out your book

The prospect of writing a book might be a bit daunting. Loads of people want to write a book, but most people don't get around to delivering on this goal. It's easier than you think, and there are people and companies out there that can help if you really don't know where to start.

You just need to start with an idea and then plan from there. Some people find it helpful to brainstorm topics around their idea and then write mini-articles on each one. With each of my books, I came up with a working title, then topics which I grouped to become sections, which gave me some structure and a framework to get started. A publisher once told me that when you have topics, you can expect to write around 1,000 words per hour. The average business book is between 30,000 and 40,000 words. In my opinion, around 36,000 is the sweet spot. Any less and the book feels a bit flimsy, any more and it becomes expensive to print and I know I'd dilute my message with waffle.

Other things to consider in the planning stage is what else you could include e.g. statistics, graphs, charts, quotes, case studies etc.

Getting published

You have a few options when publishing your book. You can approach a traditional publisher and pitch them the idea. You can find templates and guidance online which will show you what to include. The publisher is likely to be impressed by the size of your audience and want to see how engaged they are; if you have a solid following then highlight these numbers in your pitch. Without a solid following, you're likely to find the traditional approach challenging.

The advantage of working with a traditional publisher is the kudos and also the marketing they are likely to carry out. The disadvantages include them having a view on your content and the length of time it takes to get the book out.

At the other end of the scale, you can self-publish. This method has the advantages of being quick, giving you full control of the content and allowing you to retain all profits. The downside could be the quality, and you might still want to bring in support for the cover design and a proofread as a minimum. Your book represents your brand, so you don't want it to be poor quality.

There is a middle option: working with a hybrid publisher. This has a cost, either a one-off fee or a fee plus a percentage of future royalties – check the terms to understand the full commitment. The advantages of this approach are that you should end up with a good quality book you can be proud of that retains much of your original content and gets from idea to bookshelf quickly.

With my first two books, I worked with a hybrid publisher that charged a fee and takes a percentage of royalties. For the book you are holding, I published it via my own company, Moja Publishing, a hybrid option with a one-off fee.

Promoting your book

If you self-publish or go with a hybrid publisher, you're going to need to take the lead on promotion. You could hire an agency to do this for you, but if you decide to go for it yourself, my suggestion would be that you include the following in your strategy:

- Hold at least one book launch party.

- Consider a book tour.

- Create a PR plan to target local and national press.

- Approach relevant podcasts to appear as a guest to tie in with the publication date.

- Craft a social media plan.

- Start an Amazon bestseller campaign.

Consider sending copies to any influential people you know, as they will probably post on their social media and tag you. For maximum impact, you could time this around any launch activity you carry out.

The benefits of publishing a book should last for years. You can send it out to prospects or parcel it up with any speaking engagements or development programmes you run. Get creative and let me know if you come up with any ideas I've not yet thought of!

Take action

If you decide now is the right time for you to write your book, the best way to make that happen is to commit to it publicly. On your social media platform of choice, post that you are writing your book, give a little insight into the topic – if you know! – and a likely publication date. Then get writing!

Chapter Six

Board Influence

G aining more influence in your sector, city and beyond can massively boost your profile – which helps you attract even more fun opportunities.

In this chapter, I'm going to tell you why getting on a board that's not your own can be rewarding in so many ways. I'll then show you the steps you can use to identify and find board opportunities that will be right for you, along with how to apply and get offered the role.

As a business owner or senior executive, you've probably got some experience of being on a board – your own. But have you thought about joining the board of a charity or another business? You might think you haven't got time to give to someone else's board when you're busy growing your own business, but there are so many reasons why you should give it some thought.

Still need convincing?

Four reasons you should join a board

1. To make a difference

There are loads of charities and businesses of different sizes that are looking for trustees or non-executive directors. It's a great opportunity to support a cause you care about while sharing your own skills and expertise to make a difference.

2. To take on a development challenge

You will meet cool people and not-so-cool people and take learning from both. Seeing how others act in the boardroom and working with people who are experts in fields you are less experienced in will expand your own learning. We can easily become too siloed in our own environments, so working in another will challenge your thinking and perspective, which can help you to grow your own business.

3. To grow your profile

Being on a board gets your name in front of a new, and probably considerable, audience. You'll likely be tagged in (or create) various posts on social media and get featured in press articles. It adds variety to your CV and accomplishments, making it easier for you to get known among your peers and beyond.

4. To achieve an additional income stream

This shouldn't be the driver for your application, and most charity roles will be voluntary, but once you have a few under your belt, you might be tempted to apply for a paid role. These provide the benefits already listed but have the added bonus of pay and/or equity. Typical pay for a start-up NED role would be between £10,000 and £25,000 per year for a time commitment of around one day per month. Fees increase dramatically at the other end of the scale, with base fees for a FTSE 100 NED between £100,000 and £300,000, with additional fees for each committee position.

If you discover the opportunities that you're passionate about and make a positive impact, joining a board is more than worth it. When it comes to finding a role, there are two options: you can either look at joining the board of a charity – the title this usually gives you is *trustee* (the same type of role within another business is usually called a *non-executive director*). Essentially, there's no actual difference between either of these job titles.

Let's talk legal obligations...

There is a key distinction between *non-executive* and *executive*. In your non-executive role, you should be providing independence, scrutiny, support for the executive team and offering a constructive challenge. You're there to hold the executive team to account, but not "do the doing" – a trap new trustees and non-execs can easily fall into!

There is also a legal responsibility when taking on a trustee or NED role where you will be listed at Companies House and be responsible for the business and its future sustainability and growth. With a charity, you'll also be listed at the Charities Commission. This is a significant liability for a role in which you have little contact time with the organisation, are likely to be removed from the day-to-day operations and have infrequent contact with your fellow directors. So, when seeking out board opportunities make sure you do your due diligence so you know what you're letting yourself in for. Don't just accept the first role that pops up, as you could find yourself in a poor governance situation. You've got your rep to protect. Any scandal created by the company will impact on you, and we can all think of companies who have generated negative press – nobody wants that.

The upside can be benefitting from the association. If the charity or business you sit on the board of is doing great things, you'll enjoy the benefits of that – including it being super easy to have conversations with people you want to speak to and being invited to fun events.

Corporate governance is the system through which companies are directed and controlled. Boards of directors are responsible for the governance of their companies. The shareholders' role in governance is to appoint the directors to satisfy themselves that an appropriate governance structure is in place.

Typically, a company might have a board structure as follows:

- The chair – often non-executive – who oversees the whole business.

- A managing director – employed by the company – who runs the business and draws a salary. The managing director reports to the chair and oversees the board of executive directors.

- A team of executive directors who sit on the board, draw salaries and manage key areas of the business, such as finance, sales and operations.

- A team of non-executive directors who advise on the strategic direction of the business and decide remuneration of executive directors. These may be paid roles.

Ready to take on a trustee or NED role that will be worth your time?

The eight steps to securing a NED role

Step 1: Do your research

If you don't know of any board opportunities available, visit sites like LinkedIn and Indeed to learn about and search for opportunities. There are some dedicated websites that list board opportunities and give advice, such as In Touch

Networks. Large organisations and public sector roles are usually advertised in the national press, so sign up for all relevant alerts.

Step 2: Take your time

Don't jump in on the first board opportunity you see. Ask yourself, what industries would benefit the most from your skills and expertise? Then consider what type of company appeals to you, is it a non-profit, public or private sector?

Step 3: Align with your own values and aims

Take your time to find one that really aligns with your own values and aims. Not only will it be more enjoyable, but you'll be more likely to get through the selection process as genuine enthusiasm is hard to fake.

Step 4: Consider your skills and expertise

When you do find the one that you want, do your research and search existing board members. Knowing who else is on the board will give you a sense of whether you're a good fit. Do your skills and expertise complement other board members or is there an overlap?

Step 5: Understand the time commitment

Don't underestimate the time commitment. Ten days per year is typical, but some roles may require significantly more. The time required should be listed in the vacancy advert, but ask questions about this at interview or reach out to existing board members to learn more about the role. It's not just rocking up for the meetings, there'll be reading to do and possibly ongoing projects you might get involved in.

Step 6: Update your CV

If you're a business owner or you've been with the same company for a long time, you probably haven't got a current CV, or it will need some serious updating. I have a fab CV template that will ensure you capture all the useful information and present it in the right way. You'll find a link to that in the 'Resources' section, at the back of the book.

Step 7: Sort out your LinkedIn profile

Make sure it is up to date in the same way you've done with your CV. Pay special attention to where you can highlight specialist skills that are relevant to the roles you're applying for. It's worth getting some recommendations that highlight the skills you say you have. You can also use your LinkedIn profile to show you're looking for a trustee or non-exec role.

Step 8: Interview prep

Again, it might have been some time since you've been in an interview situation. The interview you have for one of these roles is likely to be with more than one interviewer – extra scary. You can prepare for these by researching the company or charity and thinking about the questions they're likely to ask. You can practise with a mock interview with a colleague or friend, or get in touch with a company like mine who offer this as a service.

Top tip

Prepare a few really good questions to ask them at the end of the interview that showcase your knowledge and enthusiasm for the role. A classic I like to use is to ask them what they most enjoy about the company. This question helps build rapport and allows them to talk about themselves which they will also probably rather enjoy.

Take action

Get board-ready! Check that your CV and LinkedIn profile are current and ready to share with a prospective recruiter. If you're not sure if yours is good enough, ask a colleague or friend to review.

Crafting a board-level CV

Ideally, you want a "board version", rather than your normal CV. If you're a business owner, you might be starting from scratch. It's useful to have a CV anyway as it is sometimes requested when bidding for work or for accreditations and further qualifications.

Contact details

Have these at the top, ideally in the header, to make the best use of space. Include your name, phone number, email address and LinkedIn profile link.

Don't include a photo if you're in the UK but if you're outside of the UK it's sometimes customary, so choose a professional headshot.

Board profile

Next up, include three to four lines for your board profile. This section should briefly summarise your board experience (non-exec and exec level) and how long you've been working with or on boards.

Board and committee experience

List your non-executive board experience, starting with your most recent first and working backwards. This can include any committee or sub-committee experience, along with any other formal responsibilities that had a strategic or governance perspective.

Executive experience

After the board experience section, you should include your executive experience. This section should also be in descending order and cover your executive career roles, including any key achievements in each one. Try to avoid the day-to-day detail of your roles, instead focusing on governance and strategic experience.

Qualifications, memberships and accreditations

List tertiary qualifications and any professional development you have undertaken. Following your formal qualifications, list any professional memberships (including grade), special interest groups, languages spoken and any other relevant activities which might be valuable in a board role.

Additional professional activities and interests

This final section adds further personality to your CV. Additional professional activities are things undertaken outside of your professional roles, but not purely social activities. For example, you could have presented at conferences, written papers, won an award or written a book. You can also include a little detail on your personal life here e.g.

referring to your love for running and the recent race you completed.

Make it clear that references are available on request, but do not include the detail of these within the CV.

Volunteering

If you don't feel ready to step into a board role right now but think you might in the future, it's worth exploring volunteering opportunities.

I secured my first external board role aged 36. In hindsight, I wish I'd gone for one earlier. I always saw these roles as something older people did, but diversity of age would actually be a valuable strength on any board. Although I was late to the (board) table, I've volunteered since my early twenties. Initially, this was with the Samaritans, where I was a listening volunteer and then also a day leader and trainer. This was a great role to do then, as it developed my communication skills and also my understanding of some of the circumstances other people find themselves in – giving me the great gift of perspective. I enjoyed working with other volunteers in this role and met people of all ages and backgrounds. I volunteered with the Samaritans for about six years, working in both the Newcastle and London Soho branches.

When I moved back to Newcastle, I took on a voluntary role with the council to support them with their adult learning provision before moving into that board role at 36, which was for five years with Age UK Northumberland as committee lead and vice chair. I then did another vice chair role for a local charity before moving into my current role as chair of Smart Works Newcastle, which is literally my dream charity role.

You'll see from my trajectory that I didn't go into a chair role immediately and that I built up my experience. That's not always the case – some people will walk into a chair role from the off. What I hope to do is show that there are a variety of voluntary roles which will deepen your experience outside of your own organisation, give you exposure to other key players in your local area and have a positive impact.

Take action

Do some research and see what opportunities are available. Ideally, you want to compile a shortlist of charities and/or companies that you'd love to work with. Then, be patient until they have an opportunity!

Being on external boards and volunteering has brought so much positivity to my life. I've supported excellent causes and businesses as well as having the privilege to meet brilliant people. These experiences have developed me as a businesswoman and provided excellent profile-raising opportunities as a bonus.

Chapter Seven

Networking Ninja: The Power Of Connections

N etworking: A word that may fill you with dread. Or maybe not, depending on how much you like people. Overall, I'm a fan of it, although my energy comes from in-person interactions, so I tend to give online networking, other than social media, a bit of a swerve.

You might not instantly think of networking when it comes to boosting your personal brand, but it's an essential component of your strategy and works well with the other methods in this book.

How does networking help raise your profile?

Networking can be a cost-effective way of raising your profile as well as meeting potential clients, collaborators and funders, especially early on in your business or career journey. As you progress your career, your networking strategy needs to evolve at the same pace. Your network needs to be different, because you need to consider who you want to raise your profile with. That's going to impact where you network and how frequently.

When you're early on in your career, you might network a lot, especially the free stuff. But as you increase your social capital, more people will invite you to events and you'll need to get choosy, otherwise you'll never get anything else done!

Regularly attend events to grow your connections

Great things can happen when you attend networking events, and the exciting part is it is often pot luck. I've attended events that were rubbish, like the one where I got stuck by the coffee table chatting to an old accountant who preferred networking sessions for golf. Get to the right events and you could strike gold.

A few years back in my first business, I was sat at an industry networking event and got chatting to a lady who was a graduate recruitment manager for a big insurance company. When I told her what my previous business was known for – large-scale mock assessment centres – she mentioned that her uncle was a professor at a North West university who was looking at doing exactly this activity with his students. One introduction later, and Bob's your uncle (actually he was called Gary). We ended up winning an annual contract with his students worth multiple six-figure sums over the contract lifetime.

There have been events I've not seen the obvious value of attending, but have led to excellent chance conversations and, ultimately, sales. Recently, I was asked to speak at the launch of a local "women in business" awards. I was happy to support it, having been a previous winner, but was only expecting a nice morning out. I got talking to the other speaker over lunch and she indicated she would be interested in our services at Moja. Fast forward a couple of months, a meeting, a proposal and a follow-up call, and we signed her up as a retainer client.

Another great example was at a charity event where I saw the owners of an activewear brand give the charity ambassador, a *Dragon's Den* Dragon with a large social media following, a branded cap. Said Dragon often wears that cap on Instagram, giving priceless exposure to the brand.

The point of these examples? You've got to be in it to win it. It's a bit like dating: Are you going to meet the partner of your dreams if you stay in the house watching Netflix by yourself every night? Nope. You have to be out there meeting lots of different people, on- or offline.

A word of caution though. Although it's wise to have goals for what you want to get from networking, if you go in too hard for sales, it might have the opposite effect. People hate the hard sell. Using the dating analogy above, you wouldn't propose to someone on the first date, so take time to build relationships. They will buy when the time is right.

The elevator pitch

When asked about your role, do you have an elevator pitch to make an impactful introduction? You've probably heard of the concept of the elevator pitch. It's a 30–60-second synopsis of your background, experience and purpose. It gets its name because the length of time it takes you to deliver your pitch is around the same time you might spend in an elevator (or *lift* if you're in the UK). I've never actually given a pitch in an elevator, but I have given a short pitch like this so many times I couldn't even estimate the number. More likely locations tend to be when giving brief introductions at a function or at the coffee table at a networking event. My mate Natalie is an expert networker. On more than one occasion, she's pitched when sat next to someone on a plane (no escape!) and won business.

The elevator pitch is the one you use in casual settings, and should be your default answer to the question, what do you do?

- The objective is merely to spark enough interest in the listener for them to be interested in continuing a conversation.

- Your pitch should *not* contain your entire value proposition. If you put too much into it, you will sound like you're desperate and selling. Be cool.

- Keep your elevator speech short and sweet, aiming to deliver your message in sixty seconds or less.

- Say who you are, what you do, and what you want to achieve.

- Be positive and persuasive with your time. Focus on the positives.

- Deliver your speech to a friend or record it, so that you can be sure that your message is clear.

If you can nail the timing on your pitch, you might want to put it in your LinkedIn profile as a pinned post. Most people don't do this, so it's worth doing it to stand out.

If your elevator pitch needs work, I've created a template you can download to craft a slick pitch. You'll find a link to that at the back of the book.

Take action

Craft or review your elevator pitch. Test it out with a trusted friend or colleague and refine it according to their feedback.

What to do before an event

Some event websites will show you who is attending in advance of the event, so take time to research and see who you'd like to make sure you speak to.

Search for the hashtag for the event or look at the posts from the organiser. Look at who is commenting and engaging and make sure you do the same. Start conversations beforehand, breaking the ice and allowing you to arrange pre-meetings. This improves the ROI on your networking and makes you more committed to attending and making the most of the event.

Top tip

Build a relationship with the host, then you know you'll have at least one great connection. You can also tell them who you'd love to speak to, and they can easily make this introduction for you.

How to make yourself memorable at the event

Making yourself stand out for all the right reasons is a great tactic to give you a good return on your networking efforts. A few ways you might do this are:

Know your limits with booze!

This is especially important when it's free drinks. Some people drink for Dutch courage (or because there's a free bar), but it leads to bad behaviour. There's someone that immediately springs to mind when I consider this point. A woman I knew from the network I had during my first business was renowned for getting completely smashed at industry events. A client of mine told me that her behaviour at events was the reason he didn't want to work with her. He felt it was too high risk in social situations. I rarely drink these days, especially at work events, but when I do, I try to follow a two-drink rule. If I go beyond two drinks, not only will it negatively impact my sleep, but it's more likely to lead to me saying something stupid.

Be colourful

There's a lot of suits at events, especially more corporate events. So if you can wear something colourful, providing you feel comfortable doing so, then you will instantly be more memorable. This is useful for follow-ups too; you can refer to yourself as 'the woman with the pink suit' or 'the guy with the orange tie'.

Adding value

Go networking, not with the mindset of what you can get from people, but with a plan of what you can give. How can you share your knowledge or become known as someone who facilitates great introductions? Every time you make an introduction that leads to a sale or collaboration, you become more known as someone adding value. This is going to lead to business karma, as people will want to do something helpful in return, when the opportunity arises.

Networking essentials

In Episode 2 of *Beyond the Bio* I spoke to networking expert, Jeni Smith, who shared what was in her bag each time she goes out networking. Here's what she takes:

- a hairbrush

- mints (useful after coffee or stinky canapes)

- a branded magnetic name badge. Not all events have these, and they make it easier for people to approach you and remember your name

- digital and traditional business cards

- a notebook to record the date, location, and host. Use this to take a note if you've said you will introduce someone. This allows you to follow through on everything you said you'd do at the event. This all links back to your invisible PR! You want to be known as someone who does what they say they will.

Top tip

Assign a notebook purely for networking. This will allow you to keep track of events, contacts and actions more easily. It will also be a useful resource for you to evaluate the success of your networking endeavours when you take time to reflect.

Following up

How do you follow up with people you have met at networking events? You need to do this fairly quickly, so they'll remember you. Did you agree on a follow-up action, such as arranging a coffee? If so, get that email across with some date options. If it was vaguer, a polite LinkedIn invitation to connect referencing where you met them will do the trick. This is another reason to be consistent on social media, so you remain relevant and in their feed for when there might be an opportunity to work with them or partner in some other way.

Do *not* under any circumstances try to sell in a LinkedIn connection request or follow-up email if you have not had any discussion that would lead you to think this is OK. All that is likely to happen is that they decline the connection request and don't get back to you. Ever. Going back to the dating analogy, you don't propose on the first date. You have to romance them a bit before you go in heavy, so don't be that person.

Top tip

Take a screenshot that shows the names of all attendees. This gives you a list to connect with easily after the event. You can do this at in-person events with table plans or attendee lists. I've massively grown my LinkedIn network by taking this approach; it can be time consuming, but it means you are adding great quality connections to your network.

Accountability and mastermind groups

A great way of networking that's a bit different is to join an accountability or mastermind group. A mastermind group is typically between five and eight people who form a group that can meet in person or online. You can meet as often as you like depending on the needs of members but, because of the group nature, a commitment is required. This commitment is crucial for your success and the success of the group as a whole.

In a mastermind, the agenda belongs to the group, and each person's participation is key. Your peers give you feedback, help you brainstorm new possibilities and set up accountability structures that keep you focused and on track. One of the biggest benefits of joining a mastermind group is that you create a community of supportive colleagues who will brainstorm together and gain tremendous insights that can improve your business. By aligning yourself with people at a similar stage in their business journey as you, you will have access to their network. You will find they naturally connect you to people who are useful, as you will do for them. Win-win.

I've been involved in several mastermind groups over the years. Most have been female only and one has been mixed sex, and I've had different support and learning from each one. With single sex groups, I've found the vibe is different. I've always gelled more with certain members that have gone on to become friends and I share more personal information in this environment. That's just me though, you might have a different experience. Try out a few options and see what works for you.

Whatever the make-up, the beauty of mastermind groups is that participants raise the bar by challenging each other to create and implement goals, brainstorm ideas and support each other with total honesty, respect and compassion. Mastermind participants act as catalysts for growth, devil's advocates and supportive colleagues.

Here's what you'll get from setting up or joining a group:

- an instant and valuable support network

- solutions and ideas, which come from brainstorming with the group

- the experience and skills of others

- increased confidence that you've made the right decisions and are taking the right actions to achieve your goals

- accountability and real progress in your business and personal life

- a sense of shared endeavour

- a boost to your confidence and motivation. You'll feel energised after every meeting

- motivation to achieve and exceed your goals

- the opportunity to celebrate success with the group

Thinking of setting up your own group?

The success or failure of a group is directly related to the skill and knowledge of the facilitator. Someone capable of running focused meetings, holding the group accountable and brainstorming with the members to find solutions to business challenges will enhance the group. If you're putting together your own group, you may want to take on this role.

Consider who you invite to the group and how many members you'll have. Not everyone will be able to make every meeting, so you need enough members to allow every meeting to go ahead even with a few no-shows, but not so many that you don't have enough time for each member.

In the groups I've been in, I find it adds an interesting dynamic to have a range of industries and backgrounds represented. You don't want to be masterminding with the competition after all! The first group I joined was all business owners and there was variation in where we were all at with our businesses. A couple of members were in their first year of trading and others had more experience.

There are pros and cons to being at different stages. My steer would be not to be the person with the most successful business. If you *are* that person, you'd be better off offering a mentoring service to new business owners – if you want to give back – and joining a mastermind with people at a similar level. Having people in your group who are doing better than you is motivating. You can see where they are and aspire to reach the same level, or exceed it if you're competitive!

The role of the mastermind group facilitator

A mastermind group facilitator is the person who'll run the group and bring out the success of every member. It's their job to create trust and rapport, help the group coach and advise each other, assist members in creating powerful goals, and hold them accountable for getting things done. In mastermind group meetings, they guide the discussion to deeper levels and manage any problems that may threaten the harmony of the group.

Before agreeing to let any new applicants into your group, it's important to screen them to make sure they'll fit in and that their commitment level is high. Decide in advance how many people should be in your group and whether empty seats will get filled. You can adopt a screening process for new members. Some questions you may wish to ask interested participants could include:

- Do you have a business vision statement?

- What are your two-year goals?

- What is your commitment to moving forward in your career or business and personal life?

- Why should you be chosen to participate in this group?

If you're setting up a new group, you could use the same set of questions. Even with a screening process, your group is likely to come across people who say that they're committed but then don't participate, or those who fail to keep the trust of the group. Be prepared to ask people to leave who aren't participating up to the acceptable standard. Do that quickly once the poor behaviour becomes evident. A *slacker* will bring down the energy and fun level for everyone.

Having a set of guidelines or a mastermind contract you all sign up to can be helpful to keep the group on track and be a clear marker of the commitment expected.

The cost of networking

Your time is the biggest investment in networking. Alongside that, you'll have travel costs, event tickets, and maybe memberships too. Often, less is more. You'll need to start by identifying what your networking objectives are. Is it access to knowledge? Sparking innovative ideas? Finding new clients? Raising your profile?

By identifying your networking goals and target audience, you can start thinking about where these people are likely to hang out. Speak to people you already know in these networks and ask them which events they rate.

Volunteering, which I covered in the previous chapter, is also a great way to network. You'll meet people who have similar values and interests, and you'll also find great content you can share on social media and beyond.

It's really important to recharge after attending a networking event. They can be unbelievably draining, so make sure you don't book in a load of meetings on the same day.

Finding good networking opportunities

Depending on your industry, you might be overwhelmed by seemingly relevant networking options. Or you might have the opposite problem if you're in a new area or niche industry.

Eventbrite

I love Eventbrite as it's so easy to search for events by location and topic. Have a play around with it to make a long list of potential events, then use websites and social media to shorten the list. Decide which ones to invest your time and money in.

Industry associations

There'll always be relevant events taking place in your industry, e.g. CIPD for HR, or the CIM for Marketing. Make friends with key people in these associations to learn first about their events and ask them to recommend anything else you might benefit from attending.

Ask your current network

I've spotted some effective shout-outs from people searching for relevant events on LinkedIn in particular. People usually have to be pretty happy with something to recommend it, so you're likely to receive good-quality suggestions to any request you make in this way.

Industry conferences

Research relevant conferences for your industry. You'll usually be able to read the agenda before attending, and in some cases, might even have access to a delegate list.

Look at local business publications

Every region has business press, and they usually host events or know about good ones to attend. Find out who the relationship manager is at these publications and let them know the events you'd love them to tell you about.

Chamber of Commerce websites

Each area in the UK has a local Chamber of Commerce. They host multiple events every month. With many of those, you'll need to be a member to attend (which could be worthwhile, depending on your business), but there are also a few free ones.

Host your own!

Can't find any great events? Consider hosting your own. Although this can be hard work, having the option to curate your own content and control the guest list will lead to so many brilliant opportunities.

Do people tell you at events or over the phone that they already know who you are through your social presence? Cringe as it sounds, this happens to me quite a bit. This shows the power of being visible using all the methods I talk about in this book. Remember the story I told in the introduction? I was pitching via Zoom during covid to a big utility company. They were a bit giggly at the start of the call, saying they felt like they were talking to a celebrity. I nearly burst out laughing when I realised they meant me! They said they felt like they knew me through social media. Although it was a bit bonkers, it made the pitch so much easier as they were a lot warmer through feeling that we'd already interacted. This highlights the value of maintaining a consistent presence on social media.

Whether you're an introvert or extrovert, I hope that I've given you some encouragement to get out there and network. Remember to be open to opportunities that come your way and start saying yes to invitations so you can assess which events work best for you.

Chapter Eight

Making It Online

B uilding a thriving online presence makes it easier for your audience to find you, and who doesn't want that? In this chapter, I'll tell you what you need to know to build your online presence and position yourself as an expert in your field. We'll look at personal websites, Google and how social media will help you get your message out there.

I've deliberately put this topic towards the end of the book as social media is what so many people think of when they're thinking of their personal brand. I see it more as the vehicle to share great content, rather than the sole method. With everything you've learned so far, social media is the icing on the cake. This chapter will get you more confident in the methods, and when and how to use them.

Personal websites

Let's start with a personal website. Isn't that for the egotistical individuals who love the limelight, the wannabe celebs of business?

Nope.

A personal website helps you build your brand and makes it easy for your audience to find and get to know you. It showcases the knowledge and expertise you've gained over your career and positions you as an expert in your field. It's also a great place to host media you're featured in, award recognition, podcasts, blogs and case studies. It can even be used to introduce you as a speaker and open up an alternative income stream through paid speaking engagements.

You might be thinking, 'I have no idea how to build a website; I'm no tech expert.' Well, you don't need to be.

There are many website builders out there – varying in degrees of difficulty and price – for you to choose from, such as Wix, WordPress and Squarespace. If you have no interest in coding and want a readymade template that you can easily customise, then Squarespace is the platform for you. If that still fills you with dread, get someone to build it for you.

Once you've built and published your website, you need to get it on Google, and I don't mean four or five pages in; it needs to be on page 1, as no one looks beyond the first page, right?

SEO is a minefield, but thankfully there's lots of information out there about SEO and how to improve it, including keywords, backlinks and page optimisation, to name a few.

If SEO fills you with fear and keywords make your head spin, at the very least, get familiar with the basics of optimising your site for search engines through Google's Search Console. It'll measure your site's search traffic and performance, highlight issues you need to fix and shine a spotlight on your site in Google search results. All of this will help you rank on the first page of Google.

It's super easy to use and helps you:

- confirm that Google can find and crawl your site

- fix indexing problems and request re-indexing of new or updated content

- view Google search traffic data for your site to check how often your site appears in Google Search

- resolve issues when Google encounters indexing, spam or other problems on your site

- identify which sites link to your website

- troubleshoot mobile usability and other search features

So, what are you waiting for? Help your audience find everything there is to know about you in one place.

Take action

Take a look at the personal websites of some big names in your industry, or even of people who are a few steps ahead of you who have their shit together. Notice what you like or dislike about their websites. Pay attention to the layout, branding, content and messaging and use this inspiration to update or create your own.

YouTube

Before we explore social media, let's look at the second biggest search engine: *YouTube.*

If you're not already on YouTube, you need to be! Posting YouTube videos with strong keywords will help to maximise your online presence. After all, Google owns YouTube, so it makes sense that YouTube videos are displayed in Google search results.

When building your YouTube channel, start by identifying who your audience is and narrowing down your niche. This will help you plan and create content for your target audience. A great way to come up with content for your channel is to think about your audience and solve a problem they might be experiencing. We've all done it, right? Headed to YouTube for a visual guide on something we need help with. Whether it's technical advice, product reviews or how to fix something, you can guarantee YouTube has the answer.

And guess what? YouTube isn't just about solving problems; it's also a great place to host your podcast if you have one or are considering starting one. Think about it, if you want to reach a wider audience, then why wouldn't you upload it to a platform that has billions of people browsing it every day?

More people listen to content on YouTube than anywhere else. At the time of writing, YouTube has overtaken Spotify to become the largest podcast consumption platform in the US.[1] It doesn't even need to have a video for it to be successful; people don't mind listening while they're doing other things like walking, exercising, or just sitting back to relax and enjoy an episode. It's pretty easy to upload a static image to an audio file and convert it to an mp4 file. There are lots of apps available on your phone that will help you with this.

---

1. Hewitt, C. (2022) 'YouTube beats out Spotify podcast listenership platform in the US. Now what?' *Castos*. Available at: https://castos.com/youtube-beats-out-spotify-podcast-listenership-platform-in-the-us-now-what/

If you really want to include video but have limited resources, Zoom is an excellent and easy option. If you want to go one step further to guarantee sound quality, then Riverside FM is the platform for you. It even lets you export clips and teasers for social media.

The biggest mistake you can make is wasting time – start building your YouTube audience today! It won't grow on its own, so here are seven tips to help you build that all-important audience:

1. Familiarise yourself with the YouTube algorithm. It's super important as it's the system that decides which videos YouTube suggests on the 'What's up next' sidebar.

2. Carefully craft descriptions, tags and titles for relevant keywords.

3. Use timestamps in your descriptions to divide videos into sections to help viewers find what they're looking for.

4. Make your thumbnails stand out and ensure they work in tandem with the title. Canva is an excellent design tool with a free version that will help you create attention-grabbing images.

5. Organise your content using playlists. This is especially useful for a sequence of videos or if you're hosting your podcast on YouTube. As soon as one episode or video ends, the next will begin.

6. Ask viewers to subscribe to your channel.

7. Promote your YouTube channel across all your social media channels using teasers or clips.

Social media

Social media platforms are excellent tools to help you build your personal brand and reach a wider audience. Creating a well-connected online network by posting regular engaging content can bring new, exciting opportunities and influence your SEO ranking on Google. For example, when you share quality content that resonates with your audience, they share it with their audience, and that amplifies your audience further: it increases visibility, improves traffic and generates backlinks. These are social signals that notify Google that you and your website are credible, which could, in turn, support the ranking of your website and social media channels on Google.

I've no doubt you'll be very familiar with social media. You'll likely be on several platforms with a preference for one or two over the others. Social media connects millions of people all over the world and is a great way to keep in touch with friends and share and document exciting memories. It's important to represent yourself well professionally on all social media platforms. I've outlined the key do's and don'ts to help you get started.

The do's

Search for yourself on the internet

You'll be amazed by how much information is captured on the internet. Make sure there's nothing on the first or second page of the search pages that could show you in a bad light. If there is, get it removed. Also, check for images that might come from old sites you no longer use.

Cleanse your social media profiles

Getting rid of any social media content that doesn't show you in the best light is the easiest way to make sure connections, recruiters and employers don't see it. I'm not saying you need to delete all your precious memories – just remove those that are less forgiving or change your privacy settings.

Check your privacy settings

If your Facebook, Twitter (or X) and Instagram accounts aren't suitable for public viewing, make sure they're private.

Be careful what you post

You never know who might view your profiles, so don't post anything inappropriate. Keep it professional.

The don'ts

Hide

Prospective clients, employers and recruiters will want to see that you have a social media presence, so don't go completely off grid.

Post anything you wouldn't want your grandparents to see

Keep it clean. Remember, information remains on the internet for a very long time.

Connect to everybody

Think twice before accepting requests from friends on your LinkedIn account. Connections should be relevant to your industry.

Overshare

Don't post anything that you'll regret later, or that could damage your reputation, or your chances of securing the job – or client – of your dreams. Be mindful of what you share and how you share it.

Most people don't post enough and miss out on the opportunities that this can bring. The thing with regular posting is that it takes time, but it becomes quicker as you get to know your audience and you can be clever about preparing your content. I often prepare my posts during dead time, such as commuting or travelling, simply drafting posts in the notes section of my phone, ready to share at appropriate times. You can learn about how often to post and when, specifically for each platform, with a bit of research. Gary Vaynerchuk[2] is well-known in this area and has some great books and YouTube content if you'd like to explore this topic further.

Take action

There are social media superstars for every platform, so find the platform that's most relevant to you and your industry and seek out those who excel. Work out what you like about their content and let that shape your own style. Research optimum posting times and frequency for your platform choice and commit to trying it out for a month. Hopefully, that will be enough for you to see the benefits and continue.

Which social platform is the best?

Let's take a look at LinkedIn, Twitter (or X) and Instagram. I've chosen these because they're the three platforms I spend most time on. If you want to explore other platforms,

---

2. Vaynerchuk, G. (2024) *Gary Vaynerchuk*. Available at: https://garyvaynerchuk.com

please do. You have to enjoy the platforms you use, or it becomes a massive chore to spend time there and that could come across to your followers.

LinkedIn

If you're searching for a job or in B2B, LinkedIn is a useful platform to be active on. Make sure that your profile is up to date and that you have completed every section. Follow companies you would like to work for, join relevant groups and interact with posts. When you meet people at events, send them a LinkedIn invitation to connect within a day. They are more likely to accept when they remember who you are, and you can continue your conversations and start building relationships.

LinkedIn has so much value for those wanting to progress their careers or who want to run their own businesses. When I was in the corporate world, I was often approached by head-hunters. As an entrepreneur, certain posts can attract business, and I've won significant deals off the back of specific LinkedIn posts that have been spotted by my target audience.

LinkedIn is a great place to share your knowledge, gain insights and lead the conversation. Remember, it's not all about posting; you also need to engage with your audience and have meaningful conversations. Consider writing LinkedIn articles to answer a problem people in your industry are experiencing. This will soon make you the go-to person and position you as a thought leader. You may even find yourself with a 'top voice' badge, awarded by the LinkedIn gods. Simplify the process and use the copy from your YouTube videos or other content. Repurposing content will make your life *so* much easier.

In my opinion, LinkedIn is the best social media platform of them all – I love it! The organic reach is unreal, and most people who use the site are lurkers, so it's easy to be visible as a content creator.

Crafting a professional profile

Your LinkedIn profile serves as your online CV and professional showcase. Here's how to make it stand out:

- Profile photo: choose a professional, high-quality headshot that reflects your personal brand. Dress appropriately and ensure the background is clean and uncluttered.

- Headline and summary: your headline should succinctly describe your expertise and either the problem you solve or your role. Use your summary to provide a compelling overview of your professional background, skills, and career/business aspirations. Try and make this fun; LinkedIn doesn't have to be serious!

- Experience and achievements: highlight key accomplishments and experiences in each section of your profile. Use bullet points to showcase quantifiable achievements and results.

Sharing valuable content

LinkedIn is a platform for professional knowledge sharing and industry insights. Here's how to position yourself as a thought leader:

- Publishing articles: write and publish articles on topics relevant to your industry or expertise. Share insights, best practices and thought-provoking analysis to demonstrate your expertise.

- Sharing updates: regularly share updates, news articles and industry trends with your network. Add your own commentary to provide context and spark conversation.

- Engaging with content: like, comment on and share content from other users in your network. Engage in meaningful conversations and contribute valuable insights to establish yourself as a trusted authority.

Building a professional network

LinkedIn is all about building meaningful professional connections. Here's how to expand your network:

- Connect strategically: send personalised connection requests to colleagues, peers, mentors and industry leaders. Include a brief message explaining why you'd like to connect.

- Joining groups: join LinkedIn groups relevant to your industry or interests. Engage in group discussions, share valuable content and connect with like-minded professionals.

- Networking events: attend virtual or in-person networking events, conferences and webinars. Use these opportunities to meet new people, exchange ideas, and grow your network.

Leveraging LinkedIn features

LinkedIn offers a range of features to help you showcase your expertise and connect with your audience:

- Recommendations: request recommendations from colleagues and clients to validate your skills and expertise. Endorse your connections' skills in return. I wouldn't bother with the actual Skills section, as I don't think people value it, so invest time in recommendations which are more detailed and come from credible contacts.

- LinkedIn Live and Events: Host live events or we-binars on LinkedIn to share your knowledge and engage with your audience in real time.

- LinkedIn Learning: Take advantage of LinkedIn Learning courses to expand your skillset and stay updated on industry trends.

- You might want to explore LinkedIn Premium. My view on this is to try it out for a month when they offer you a free trial to have a play with the features and see if it adds value in how you use it. I've had a premium membership a few times, but it just hasn't been worth it to me so I've never renewed it.

Tracking performance and optimisation

Monitor your LinkedIn performance and optimise your strategy for maximum impact:

- Analytics: use LinkedIn Analytics to track profile views, post engagement and follower demograph-ics. Analyse your performance data to understand what content resonates with your audience.

- Optimisation: regularly optimise your profile and content based on feedback and performance met-rics. Experiment with different posting times, con-tent formats, and messaging to maximise engage-ment.

- Stay active: consistency is key on LinkedIn. Stay active by regularly sharing content, engaging with your network, and participating in discussions to maintain visibility and relevance.

Top tip

Stop reposting other people's content! You'll see, if you look at your analytics, that it has zero impact. The only caveat to this is if you're being strategic to support a client – that said, they'd benefit far more if you simply liked and commented on their post.

Twitter/X

Welcome to the world of X (even though everyone still calls it Twitter), where brevity is key and every character counts. I want to show how you can leverage the power of Twitter and connect with your audience effectively. Twitter is more conversational than the other platforms.

Crafting your profile

Your Twitter profile serves as your digital business card. It's the first impression you make on potential followers, so make it count. Here's how:

- Profile picture: choose a clear, professional photo. Avoid using logos or blurry images.

- Bio: craft a concise yet compelling bio that high-lights who you are, what you do, and what makes you unique. Use keywords relevant to your niche to improve discoverability.

- Handle: your Twitter handle (username) should ideally reflect your name and/or brand. If your name is unavailable, get creative with a variation that's easy to remember.

Content strategy

Twitter moves at lightning speed, so it's essential to have a clear content strategy to cut through the noise:

- Consistency: regularly share valuable content to stay top-of-mind with your audience. Whether it's daily insights, weekly tips or timely commentary, consistency is key.

- Variety: mix up your content with a blend of text, images, videos and GIFs to keep your feed engaging and dynamic. Experiment with different formats to see what resonates best with your audience.

- Engagement: don't just broadcast; engage with your audience. Respond to comments, retweet interesting posts and participate in relevant conversations to develop meaningful connections.

Building your network

Twitter is a powerful networking tool, allowing you to connect with like-minded individuals and industry influencers:

- Follow relevant accounts: follow accounts within your industry, niche and target audience to stay informed and broaden your network.

- Join chats and hashtag conversations: participate in Twitter chats and follow popular hashtags relevant to your interests to join conversations and expand your reach.

- Engage authentically: be genuine in your interactions and avoid "spammy" tactics. Build relationships by adding value, offering insights and supporting others in your network.

Analytics and optimisation

Track your Twitter performance and optimise your strategy for maximum impact:

- Analytics: use Twitter Analytics to monitor your performance metrics, including impressions, engagements and follower growth. Analyse what's working and what's not to refine your approach.

- A/B testing: experiment with different types of content, posting times and messaging to identify the most effective strategies for your audience.

- Iterate and improve: your Twitter strategy should be dynamic and should evolve over time. Continuously monitor results, gather feedback and adapt accordingly to ensure long-term success.

You might want to consider paying for verification if you use this platform a lot. It will give you credibility, show people it is really you and give you a boost from the old algorithms, as well as access to a few extra features.

Twitter can be a powerful tool for building and enhancing your personal brand, but success doesn't happen overnight. It requires consistency, authenticity and strategic thinking. By crafting a compelling profile, sharing valuable content, building meaningful connections and optimising your strategy based on data-driven insights, you can leverage the full potential of Twitter.

Instagram

Now more than ever, people are looking for brands they can identify and engage with on a personal level. Instagram is more visual than LinkedIn and Twitter; it's a great way to show your audience what it's like behind the scenes, an insight into your life, allowing you to connect with your audience in a meaningful way. Use stories and reels to share instant news and help them visualise what you have to offer.

In the visual world of Instagram, captivating imagery and engaging storytelling reign supreme. This is a platform I've been inspired to make more effort to understand after I interviewed yoga teacher Jo Hutton about going viral in Episode 37 of *Beyond the Bio*.

Creating an eye-catching profile

Your Instagram profile is your digital storefront, so it's essential to make it visually appealing and reflective of your personal brand:

- Profile photo: choose a high-quality, recognisable photo of yourself or your brand logo as your profile picture. Ensure it's clear and visually appealing even when displayed in a small circle.

- Bio: craft a concise and compelling bio that encapsulates who you are, what you do and what sets you apart. Use emojis and line breaks to enhance readability and personality.

- Link: use the single link in your bio strategically. Direct followers to your website, blog, latest project or landing page to drive traffic and conversions. If you have lots of places you'd like to send followers, explore using Linktree. The free option has good functionality, but you can pay a small monthly fee and customise it to suit.

Curating compelling content

Instagram is all about visual storytelling, so focus on creating content that resonates with your audience:

- High-quality imagery: invest in high-quality photos and videos that showcase your personality, expertise and interests. Use editing tools to enhance your visuals while maintaining authenticity – go easy on those filters!

- Consistent aesthetic: develop a consistent visual theme or aesthetic for your feed to create a cohesive and memorable brand identity. Whether it's through colour schemes, filters, or content themes, consistency is key.

- Diverse content mix: mix up your content with a variety of formats, including photos, videos, carousels, stories and reels. Experiment with different content types to keep your feed engaging and fun.

Engaging your audience

Instagram is a social platform, so prioritise engagement and interaction with your audience:

- Respond to comments: take the time to respond to comments on your posts and engage with your followers. Show appreciation for their support and encourage a sense of community around your brand.

- Use stories and polls: leverage Instagram Stories to share behind-the-scenes content, polls, Q&A sessions and interactive stickers to encourage engagement and feedback from your audience.

- Collaborate and tag others: collaborate with other users, tag relevant accounts in your posts and participate in Instagram challenges and shoutouts to expand your reach and connect with new audiences.

Tracking performance and optimisation

Monitor your Instagram performance and optimise your strategy by including these suggestions for maximum impact:

- Insights: use Instagram Insights to track key metrics such as reach, engagement and follower demographics. Analyse your performance data to identify trends and opportunities for improvement.

- Test and iterate: experiment with different posting times, content formats and captions to gauge audience preferences. Continuously test and iterate your strategy based on data-driven insights.

- Stay authentic: above all, stay true to yourself and your brand. Authenticity resonates with audiences on Instagram, so be genuine in your content and interactions.

As with Twitter, you might want to consider paying for verification if you use this platform a lot. It will give you credibility, show people it's really you and give you a boost in the algorithms, as well as access to a few extra features.

Instagram, as with most of the other platforms, makes changes to its algorithms so try and keep on top of what's current. At the time of writing, reels are still hugely popular, and it was a reel that went viral that took Jo from 2,500 followers to 168,000. I was so inspired by her experience that I've committed to posting more educational reels myself. If you follow me (@moja_sophie) and I'm not being consistent, this is your cue to give me a prod!

There are other social platforms, such as Facebook and TikTok. Do your research to identify where your audience hangs out to connect with them in a meaningful way. Ask yourself, do I need to be on one platform or several?

Consistency is key

Spoiler alert, it's pretty easy to be inconsistent and drop off the face of the earth, resulting in zero online presence.

Top tips

To stay visible, here are my general top tips:

- Post regularly to keep your pages populated with your latest ventures.

- Use video clips and teasers to promote content on your YouTube channel and increase subscribers.

- Google takes time to update its ranking, so stay consistent and keep your profile active.

- Post any media coverage you get to entice people and help you move up the rankings.

The easiest and most effective way to have a strong personal brand is via social media. As I said earlier, it's best to stick to one or two platforms. If you spread yourself too thinly, it can be hard to keep up with them all – trust me, I've tried! I made the choice to focus mostly on LinkedIn and Twitter initially, as that's where my audience spent most of their time. I would try to post on Twitter a few times a day and on LinkedIn twice a week.

A few things happened that made me realise I had nailed these two platforms. First, my connections and followers started growing quickly, but more importantly, so did the engagement on my posts. A good LinkedIn post these days on my profile will get 30,000–50,000 views, which is certainly above average. The other thing I noticed was that when I was out and about meeting clients, they often referred to something I had posted about e.g. 'Well done on winning that award last week – I saw it on LinkedIn.' I have a couple of funny stories that highlight the progress I made on these platforms. The first was on LinkedIn when a guy I vaguely knew asked me to promote a product he was selling and called me an influencer. The second is even more hilarious.

A couple of years ago I was walking down Pink Lane in Newcastle on the way to a meeting at Pink Lane Coffee. As I was walking downhill towards the coffee shop, I spotted this tiny blonde lady outside chatting on the phone and waving at me frantically. My eyesight was pretty good back then, so even from a distance I knew I did not know this lady. As I walked closer, she became more animated, and I had to make a quick decision – should I pretend I knew her or come clean? I decided to come clean.

'I'm so sorry but I have absolutely no idea who you are,' I said in my best friendly voice.

The lady, Kate, replied, 'Oh my god, I'm so embarrassed. I follow you on Twitter and just feel like I totally know you!'

We had a good laugh, which broke the ice and I asked her about what she did. Both of us were off to separate meetings in the same coffee shop, but we swapped cards and arranged to meet for a coffee another time.

On meeting up a few weeks later, I learned that Kate delivered the training for coaching qualifications (among other things), and I ended up completing my Level 7 coaching and mentoring qualification with her, where I got to know her better. We've since been in two mastermind groups together and become friends.

These days Instagram has overtaken Twitter in relevance for me, but my love for LinkedIn is still strong. Find your platform and stick with it.

Take your time

Consistency isn't just about the volume of posts you put out. It's about your whole look. While you might have a slightly different vibe on each platform, you want anyone visiting your profile to be able to tell it's you immediately, no matter the platform. An easy way of doing this is to use the same profile picture across all social media platforms so you're instantly recognisable.

Don't feel like you need to master every platform and post every day immediately. It's easier (and more fun) to start with one or two and nail them before considering being present everywhere. Some people are fans of repurposing content across all platforms, which feels like a good use of time. I think that works better across company profiles, which (usually) people don't pay too much attention to anyway. With personal profiles, it is more obvious when you try that approach. Whatever tactics you employ, remember to set goals and look at the analytics. If it isn't working, change things up!

There we are, some tips and tricks to help increase your online visibility. It's time to get your name out there, create brand trust and build your reputation in your industry and beyond. After all, people do business with people they know, like and trust. You've learned the tools and tricks – now it's time to take action that will deliver results.

Chapter Nine

Bringing It All Together: Action-Planning

You've made it to the end of *From Unknown to Unforgettable*, so I'm hoping you've gained valuable insights into networking, awards, press and media engagement, board influence, authority building, maximising speaking opportunities and enhancing your online visibility.

Now, armed with knowledge and inspiration, it's time to translate these insights into actionable plans that propel you towards your professional goals. In this final chapter, I'm highlighting the value of action planning, guiding you through the process of setting strategic objectives, identifying key actions and implementing a roadmap for success.

Setting clear objectives

The foundation of any action plan lies in setting clear and achievable objectives. Start by defining your overarching goals, whether it's to expand your network, increase media visibility, secure a board position or become a recognised authority in your field. Break these goals down into Specific, Measurable, Attainable, Relevant and Time-bound (SMART) objectives that provide clarity and focus.

Example objective

> **Goal:** Enhance Online Visibility.
> **SMART Objective:** Increase LinkedIn engagement by 30 per cent within six months by posting thought leadership content bi-weekly, engaging with industry influencers and participating in relevant LinkedIn groups.

When setting objectives, it's essential to consider not just the outcome you wish to achieve, but also the resources, timelines and potential challenges involved. By making your objectives specific and measurable, you can track progress effectively and make adjustments as needed.

Identifying key actions

Once you've established your objectives, identify the key actions necessary to achieve them. Use the strategies and tactics outlined in previous chapters to your advantage. Tailor your actions to align with your objectives, emphasising activities that are likely to yield the greatest impact and align with your strengths and resources.

Example key actions

ACTIVITY	ACTION
Networking	Attend two industry conferences and three networking events per quarter to expand your professional circle and add new connections.
Media engagement	Pitch three guest article ideas to industry publications and schedule monthly media interviews to share expertise and increase visibility.
Authority building	Publish one thought leadership article per month on your personal blog or LinkedIn, addressing trending topics in your field and showcasing your expertise.
Speaking opportunities	Apply to speak at two industry conferences and host a webinar series on niche topics within your domain to establish credibility and reach new audiences.
Online visibility	Optimise your LinkedIn profile with relevant keywords, update your website with recent achievements and testimonials, and engage with your audience regularly through blog posts and social media updates.

Each key action should be aligned with specific objectives and contribute to their achievement. It's essential to prioritise actions based on their potential impact and feasibility, considering factors such as time, resources and expertise required.

Developing a roadmap

With your objectives and key actions defined, it's time to map out a detailed plan of action. Create a timeline that outlines specific milestones, deadlines and responsibilities, ensuring accountability and progress tracking. Break your actions into manageable tasks, assigning resources and deadlines for each step of the process. Stay flexible and adaptable, allowing room for adjustments as needed while maintaining focus on your ultimate objectives.

I've created a handy roadmap template, which (alongside a lot of other useful things) you'll find in the Resources section at the back.

Example roadmap

MONTH	ACTIVITY
1	• Research and select industry conferences and networking events to attend. • Draft guest article pitches and reach out to relevant publications.
2–3	• Attend selected conferences and events, actively engaging with peers and industry leaders. • Follow up with new connections and schedule coffee meetings to strengthen relationships.
4–6	• Secure speaking opportunities and finalise webinar topics and formats. • Publish thought leadership articles and engage with media outlets for interview opportunities.
Ongoing	• Monitor and analyse metrics related to online visibility, networking effectiveness and media engagement. • Adjust strategies and tactics based on feedback and performance data.

The roadmap serves as a guide for implementing your action plan, providing a clear timeline and allocation of resources. Regularly review and update the roadmap to adapt to changing circumstances and emerging opportunities.

Implementing and evaluating

With your action plan in place, it's time to put your strategies into motion.

Execute each task with diligence and commitment, leveraging your skills, expertise and network to achieve your objectives. Regularly monitor your progress against your predefined metrics, tracking key performance indicators and adjusting your approach as needed to stay on course. Celebrate successes, learn from challenges and continually iterate your action plan to maximise your impact and achieve your professional aspirations.

Example metrics

ACTIVITY	METRIC
Networking	Number of new connections made, quality of relationships established, and referrals generated.
Media engagement	Number of media mentions, article views, and audience engagement metrics.
Authority building	Engagement metrics on thought leadership content, website traffic and follower growth.
Speaking opportunities	Number of speaking engagements secured, audience reach, and feedback received.
Online visibility	LinkedIn profile views, website traffic, social media engagement and search engine rankings.

Regular evaluation of metrics allows you to gauge the effectiveness of your actions and make data-driven decisions for improvement. By identifying what's working well and which areas need adjustment, you can optimise your efforts for maximum impact. Remember, all of this data is also incredibly useful when it comes to those award submissions.

Take action for lasting impact

As you embark on the journey outlined in this book, remember that action is the catalyst for transformation. By setting clear objectives, identifying key actions, developing a roadmap and implementing your plan with purpose and perseverance, you can turn your aspirations into achievements and leave a lasting impact in your field.

You don't need to do everything right now, although I say that with tongue firmly in cheek, as someone who always wants to do everything yesterday! By identifying your priorities and creating plans, you'll ensure you stay on track while not becoming overwhelmed.

Embrace the process of continuous improvement, remain agile in the face of challenges and seize every opportunity to elevate your professional journey beyond the ordinary. Say yes to everything until you hit the point where you need to start saying no. Your actions today pave the way for more sales, collaborations and excitement in the months and years to come.

Now it's your time to get stuck in!

Remember, the journey will require commitment, resilience, and a willingness to put yourself out there. As you navigate your path, stay focused, stay motivated, and most importantly, stay true to yourself. With the tools and strategies shared in this book, you're now equipped to step into the spotlight and leave an indelible mark on your industry.

Go out there, make your impact, and transform yourself from unknown to unforgettable.

I wish you lots of luck and excitement along the way.

Resources

For ALL the resources, including:

- the values table (from chapter one)

- scorecard

- template for awards strategy

- awards entry one sheet

- board CV template

- elevator pitch

- roadmap for goal setting

visit www.fromunknowntounforgettable.com/resources

Additional resources

- Sophie's TEDx Talk: The Truth Behind The Showreel https://youtu.be/woZ_d3WTtR4

- You'll find information on workshops, events and online courses at www.thisismoja.com.

- Beyond The Bio podcast: https://rss.com/podcasts/beyond-the-bio-with-sophie-milliken/

Useful Websites

These have all been mentioned within the book, but I thought it would be handy to list them in one place:

- AnswerThePublic.com

- Bdaily.co.uk

- Chartable.com

- CoverageBook.com

- Eventbrite.com

- Google Search Console

- Grammarly.com

- Moz.com

- Qwoted.com

- Riverside.fm

- Squarespace.com

- UberSuggest.com

- Wix.com

- WordPress.com

Also by Sophie Milliken

From Learner to Earner

The Ambition Accelerator

Acknowledgements

I must thank everyone who has encouraged me to write this book, and especially to my team at Moja for holding me to account to finally get it done. To Rachael Cook, my right-hand woman, for giving me a hard deadline and basically making me just crack on. To Ava Hartington for all her epic proofreading and incredible behind-the-scenes work. To Tony Clark for the copyedit, formatting the whole book and writing some banging copy for the launch. To Lottie Steele for editing the podcast week in and week out, ensuring each polished episode is out on the day it should be... And lastly to Aaron Cook for miscellaneous podcast edits and Photoshop support.

Thank you to Sara for writing such a brilliant foreword and supporting my business journey always in so many other ways. You're a legend!

Thank you to Anna Wilk, Emma Vincent, Kirsty Waite, Tian Tang, Laura Bosworth and Jelena Djordjevic, the beta readers for committing the time to reading my first draft and giving me valuable and constructive feedback that has shaped the book you're holding right now.

Thank you to Natasha McDonough who kept telling me I had to start my own podcast and gave me that final push to get started.

Thank you to all the guests I have had the pleasure of interviewing. Far too many to name and hopefully many more to come. You've given your time and insights so generously and have helped to make the podcast the success it is.

Of course, special thanks must be given to listeners of *Beyond the Bio*. I love hearing from you when a particular episode resonates, and your thoughtful ratings and reviews help the show more than you know.

About The Author

Sophie Milliken MBE is the founder and CEO of Moja Group. Moja works with entrepreneurs and senior executives to amplify their personal profiles and become known authorities in their industries.

Moja Publishing was launched in 2024, offering publishing solutions across paperback, e-book and audiobook formats.

A multi-award-winning businesswoman and proud solo mum, Sophie enjoys living and working in the North East. She's a passionate supporter of Northern Power Women and the co-founder of City Ladies Networking.

Sophie's also chair of Smart Works Newcastle, who support unemployed women throughout the North East with interview clothing and coaching that enables them to 'get the job'.

In June 2021, Sophie became a founding ambassador for Every Child Needs a Mentor.

Sophie was awarded an MBE for services to Business and Education in the 2023 New Year honours list.